latin evolution

jose garces

latin evolution

jose garces

with april white

photography by tina rupp

tion

lake isle press

Published by:
Lake Isle Press, Inc.
16 West 32nd Street, Suite 10-B
New York, NY 10001
(212) 273-0796
E-mail: lakeisle@earthlink.net

Distributed to the trade by:
National Book Network, Inc.
4501 Forbes Boulevard, Suite 200
Lanham, MD 20706
1(800) 462-6420
www.nbnbooks.com

Library of Congress Control Number: 2008929057

ISBN-13: 978-1-891105-37-1

Book and cover design: Ellen Swandiak

Editors: Pimpila Thanaporn, Katherine Trimble

Photography: Tina Rupp; prop styling, Stephanie Basralian; food styling, Toni Brogan

This book is available at special sales discounts for bulk purchases as premiums or special editions, including customized covers. For more information, contact the publisher at (212) 273-0796 or by e-mail, lakeisle@earthlink.net

First edition

Printed in the United States of America

10 9 8 7 6 5 4 3 2 1

To four generations of Garces women:

Amada, Magdalena, Beatriz, and Olivia

acknowledgments

Without MAMITA AMADA, none of this would have been possible. Her devotion to cooking, even at age 87, is truly an inspiration. My mother, MAGDALENA, instilled in me the ambition to become a chef at a very young age. My wife, BEATRIZ, is the pillar of my success. Without her, I would not have accomplished nearly as much in the past 5 years. Her support and love of what we do is tremendous.

Chef DOUGLAS RODRIGUEZ is a mentor, a close friend, and a major source of encouragement. After working for more than five years in the business, I came to Douglas without having a clear vision for my future. I met him at his South American eatery, Chicama, in New York City, where Douglas had surrounded himself with many talented chefs: Raymond Mohan, Max Tejada, George Arizola, Adrian Leon, and Ramiro Jimenez. Douglas's contagious passion for food made him the perfect leader for us. It was there, with this ensemble of talent, that I was able to grow and to understand Latin cooking. His teachings and philosophies as they relate to food continue to shape the way I approach both ingredients and techniques. You can still see traces of Douglas's tutelage throughout the recipes written here. His guidance is a big part of who I've become.

This book would not have been possible without the help of the young, ambitious CHEFS OF AMADA AND TINTO: Chad Williams, Tim Spinner, Adriane Appleby, Dave Conn, Andrew Sabin, and Will Zuchman. Their work and commitment to our culinary philosophies and new traditions helped to shape this book. The STAFF OF AMADA AND TINTO possess a commitment to excellence without which it would have been impossible for me to take the time to write this book. Sous chef DAN SWEISFORD worked tirelessly to put these recipes on paper. KEVIN SBRAGA deserves a huge thank you for helping us to reach the finish line in testing these recipes.

The encouragement from my publicist, agent and friend CLARE PELINO and her staff at Profile PR made this book a reality. Her belief in what we do has always pushed me to do more.

MELISSA WENTZELL is our director of operations and someone who I consider to be a close friend. Her ability to stay on top of operations while also providing me with the breathing room and time to be able to complete this project was a huge help.

When I was looking for someone to co-write this book with me, the first person who came to mind was APRIL WHITE. She was a first-hand witness to my ascent in the Philadelphia dining scene, from my arrival at Alma de Cuba to the opening of Amada. April's lucid writing style, attention to detail and tenacity for ensuring that all of the recipes were consistent were great assets to this project.

Adding an academic angle, BROOKE EVERETT's research and translation skills along with her in-depth look at the historical and cultural origins of these recipes formed the backbone for *Latin Evolution*. Whether a recipe was from Spain, Latin America, or South America, Brooke approached each topic with endless curiosity and enthusiasm.

Working with HIROKO KIIFFNER, PIMPILA THANAPORN, and KATE TRIMBLE at LAKE ISLE PRESS has been one of the most pleasurable working relationships I've had to date. When I was originally pitching the concept for *Latin Evolution*, I was unsure what the reaction would be to the concept. They had the foresight and the vision to make this a dream come true for me.

Photographer TINA RUPP and her food styling crew spent countless hours on making these recipes come to life, and it was graphic designer ELLEN SWANDIAK's vision that completed this beautiful final product.

THE CULINARY TEAM AT AMADA AND TINTO. Back row, left to right: Chad Williams, Jose Garces, Tim Spinner. Front row, left to right: Andrew Sabin, Adriane Appleby, Dave Conn, Will Zuchman, Dan Sweisford.

contents

new & old world

spanish

traditions

S low-cooked lechon asado, citrusy ceviche, and a crisp-crusted, beef-filled Argentinean empanada. That may sound like dinner to you, but for me, it is a history lesson, a tasty way of understanding how the cuisines of Spain, Mexico, and much of South America developed—and how they will continue to evolve. • Let's start with Christopher Columbus and the century of Spanish conquistadors who followed him from Spain to Mexico and beyond. As every child learns in history class, Hernán Cortés conquered the Aztecs and portions of what is now Mexico for Spain in 1519. What those history classes don't always teach: Cortés conquered a people, but not their cuisine. Before the conquest, the Aztec diet was rich in corn, beans, chiles, and complex sauces made from seeds. In the 1520s, under Spanish rule, the same crops grew in abundance—and they still do. The Spaniards struggled to tame the land and the palate, growing wheat wherever possible throughout Mexico and Central America and raising grazing animals once foreign to this part of the world. They brought the cow and the pig—the beef, the pork, the lard—but they couldn't impose their tastes or recreate the Spanish diet in this new world. Instead, the Aztec appetite adapted to this Spanish influence, incorporating these newly available foods into an already rich cuisine. • In the 16th century that story repeated itself throughout the New World—in Peru, Chile, Argentina, Ecuador, Cuba, Jamaica, and Puerto Rico. The Spanish sphere of culinary influence reached as far as the region that would become the southwestern United States. (Think Tex-Mex.) By the time the empire collapsed in the 19th century, its legacy of onions, garlic, limes, lemons, and oranges was firmly entrenched. Even the now-ubiquitous sugarcane is a vestige of the Spanish; in Mexico it was grown first by the conquering Cortés. • As a chef I find this historical perspective freeing. It made me realize that how we eat is in a constant state of flux, our diets dictated less by our taste buds than by dozens of variables—economics, politics, religion, health, and weather—all as powerful, unpredictable, and unstoppable as a conquering force. Understanding that the Latin American dishes I'd always thought of as "authentic" were simply a snapshot of an ever-changing culture gave me permission to experiment with this intersection of Spanish, Mexican, and South American cuisines. Introducing new techniques and new flavors to those classics is part of a natural culinary evolution. And no cuisine can—or should be—static. • That was a lesson the Spanish appetite learned from its colonies in the New World. The Aztecs, the Incans, and other New World peoples may have been the conquered, but their crops—tomatoes, potatoes, vanilla, chocolate, honey—waged a successful invasion on Spanish cuisine. Think of some of the most "authentic" Spanish dishes, from the potato-studded tortilla Española to the tomato-rich gazpacho.

a chef's latin evolution

In thinking about this book, I kept returning to the phrase that became its title: *Latin Evolution*. It is the phrase that best describes my cooking. As a chef, my constant challenge is to see the possibilities that new ingredients and techniques offer, while honoring what has come before. My mantra is simple: "authentic" and "innovative" are not contradictory. The most advanced techniques of gastronomic science lend themselves to re-imagining even traditional dishes so long as it's done with respect for the ingredients and cuisine. This is the next chapter in the story of Latin food culture in America. • But more than that, "Latin Evolution" is a phrase that describes my own experiences; my dishes are a reflection of my own evolution, and this recipe collection is a highly personal mix of family history, culinary training, creativity, and my personality.

This is a story about me and others like me, first-generation Americans who spoke Spanish at home and English at school, people who felt like outsiders in their neighborhoods but relished the camaraderie and comfort of the family table. As an Ecuadorian kid growing up in an Irish Catholic neighborhood in Chicago, I would never have imagined that the foods I loved would become so well known and regarded. Little did I know that my earliest days spent at the stove with my grandmother, preparing the dishes that have been a part of my family for generations, would one day inform the menu items at my restaurants: Amada, Tinto and Distrito in Philadelphia, and Mercat a la Planxa in Chicago.

I first came to professional cooking as a student in Kendall College's culinary program. I had always enjoyed food and cooking, but my coursework provided the direction and focus I needed to launch a career. My final project at Kendall involved creating a business plan for a restaurant, an imaginary Spanish tapas restaurant strikingly similar to my first restaurant, Amada.

Though my earliest jobs were at non-Latin restaurants—the Signature Room in Chicago and the Rainbow Room in New York City—my heart was never far from my Latin roots. I began to explore the connections between Old World and New World cuisines as an apprentice at La Taberna del Alabardero in Marbella, Spain. As my interest in Latin food intensified, I set out to work for Douglas Rodriquez, widely regarded as the godfather of Nuevo Latino cuisine. Douglas, a master of flavors,

was doing the exciting work of introducing the United States to this "new" cuisine.

When I was finally hired to work for him at his popular New York eateries, Chicama and Pipa, it was as if I were starting my career over again as a line cook, earning just $12 an hour. I was fresh from a disappointing run as executive chef at Bolivar, also in New York. At 27, I thought I was ready to lead a kitchen, but my year there showed me otherwise. After five years of building a name for myself, it was difficult to go back to square one, but I knew it was necessary in order to become the chef I wanted to be.

I was thrilled to be cooking the kinds of food that I craved, but eventually I started to dream of opening my own Latin-inspired restaurant. When Douglas asked me to join him in Philadelphia to open Stephen Starr's Alma de Cuba, I knew it would bring me one step closer to my goal, even though it would mean leaving New York City. I had really fallen in love with the city's energetic vibe. It was a challenge and a thrill to live and work in the country's culinary epicenter, a place where many great chefs have started their careers. Yet, given this new opportunity, I knew it was time to move on. As executive chef at Alma de Cuba, my personal style of cooking evolved at a faster pace than ever before. My philosophy about food and cooking began to emerge. I started to simplify my dishes, streamlining preparations while still respecting the traditions behind them.

Though I was still working with Douglas, he wasn't on the scene every day, allowing me to take on a greater role in creating recipes and managing a restaurant. Within the repetitive cycle of cooking for daily dinner service, I really started to grow beyond just executing other people's food. Creating daily specials was part of this process, and I found that the challenge of creating my own dishes each day helped to hone my style. Many young chefs don't recognize the need for repetition and practice, but without it, it's impossible to achieve one's potential. Soon, I started the cycle again at El Vez, another Stephen Starr restaurant, where I threw myself into the world of Mexican cooking, putting my modern stamp on traditional dishes. It was then that my food philosophy and my personal style really fell into place.

throughout my professional training, my thoughts often turned back to my youth. Understanding tradition has always been very important to my family, as it is in many Latin families. Every afternoon of my childhood my mother would prepare the dishes she had learned from my father's mother. And every day, I would sit at the kitchen table to watch my mother cook. Later, I was even allowed to help make our family favorites—arepas, empanadas, and ceviches. Today, as I watch my mother teach my wife those same cooking lessons, I am constantly reminded how closely food, family, and community are connected. And this idea extends to my restaurants: I love bringing the pleasures of the table to others, and visitors to my restaurants are like guests in my home.

Traditional dishes nourished my love of cooking, and I couldn't have written a cookbook without them. But I know my grandmother wouldn't recognize many of the dishes in my restaurants or the recipes in this book. The traditions she passed on provided my frame of reference, but the classic French training I received at culinary school, my experience with master chefs, and my own creative instincts are just as important.

The chefs I admire most, including Martín Berasategui, Juan María Arzak, Daniel Boulud, Thomas Keller, Rick Bayless, Felipe Rojas-Lombardi, Paco Torreblanca, Mario Batali, Ferran Adrià, among others, have a real passion for the food they cook and a true understanding of the history behind their cuisines. When I was younger, I sometimes felt restricted by the strong traditions of my culture, but in the kitchen, those same traditions became a solid basis on which to build my own style. I've cooked many different types of food in my career and my theory has been proven true in every kitchen. If you understand the basics of a dish, you can create new, exciting riffs on that tradition. That's how my personal cuisine evolved, and it is how a shared cultural cuisine evolves as well.

The development of each dish in my repertoire begins with a simple question: what is the core of this dish? Is it the balance of textures and the touch of citrus in a Peruvian tiradito, the precise method for making a Mexican mole, the incredible quality of the Spanish octopus in pulpo gallego? My challenge is to improve the concept without changing its soul. I ask myself, can I deconstruct a complex recipe into simpler components? Can I replace a lackluster ingredient with one that is at the peak of its freshness? Can I cross culinary boundaries, finding delicious similarities among the traditions of different regions?

The process of breaking down dishes and taking a fresh look at the elements—not just their flavors, but also their shape, texture and colors—allows me to be inspired time and again by these "original" recipes. My version of basic South American shellfish ceviche, for example, uses traditional techniques while incorporating nontraditional ingredients such as black truffles, Meyer lemon, and micro arugula. The result is a dish that reflects in every bite both my heritage and my contemporary style.

And it is important to realize that culinary traditions are not limited to ingredients and techniques. Every culture also offers distinct dining traditions. The small-plate philosophy that has shaped so much of my work stems from Spanish culture. Each time I travel to Spain, this food culture calls to me even more. It's a marvelous way to enjoy a meal. I find that entrees—especially the oversize ones that have become typical fare on American menus in recent years—bring on palate fatigue. And there's nothing worse than eating those last few bites for which you are no longer hungry. Tapas is a style whose time has come in America.

There is limitless possibility in the flavors and culinary traditions of the Spanish-speaking world -- the artisanal products of Spain, the distinct complex flavors of South America and the Caribbean (especially all of those amazing chiles), and the precise cooking techniques of Mexico. Mexican cuisine is a particularly rich melting pot. The 300-year-long involvement of the Spanish, who brought the region the spices that resulted in mole, and the influence of Mayan and Aztec cultures, whose ancient ways of cooking are still used, have combined to form a cuisine that is at once contemporary and traditional. The subtle places where these distinct food cultures overlap serve as my inspirations. My version of arepas (p. 128) is a perfect example. The corn cakes, browned in sizzling vegetable oil, are similar to what you'd find from a street vendor in Ecuador—or from my mother's kitchen—but I top them with a Caribbean-inspired ropa vieja of slow-stewed oxtail, tender onions and sweet peppers. Then I dress the open-faced sandwich with two very American ingredients: crisp bacon and the freshest, most flavorful tomatoes I can find. It's a dish that would fit in a South American arepas house or an American Southern barbecue. And it's so good, it just might become a new tradition.

—Jose Garces

CHEF'S NOTE: I've presented the different elements of each dish as individual component recipes so that you may prepare and use them separately, if desired. If you are making all of the component recipes, be sure to read each one carefully to plan and organize the ingredients and their preparation.

ceviche

y tiradito

the tradition of ceviche

Bright, fresh ceviche is a staple in the Peruvian diet,

and a perfect canvas on which to experiment with

flavors from around the world. This preparation of raw

fish may seem uniquely South American, the way sushi

belongs to Japan, but it wouldn't even exist without the Spanish

conquistadors of the 16th century. The Europeans brought citrus to

the New World, and the fruits' acidity is an essential component of

ceviche. • Peruvian fisherman, loaded down with the day's catch,

were probably the first to develop this basic method of dressing

raw fish: The diced flesh is "cooked" in citrus and garnished with

easy-to-find ingredients like chiles, corn, and potatoes. The dish's

flexibility—the same thing that attracts me to it—allowed the

tradition to spread quickly through South and Central America, with each region contributing its own flavors. • In my kitchen, I have access to many more ingredients than those early fisherman—briny West Coast oysters, sweet Nantucket Bay scallops, Japanese hamachi, even high-quality duck and in-season artichokes—but my approach to ceviche is the same: the freshest ingredients with a simple marinade. I've created a basic marinade of lime juice with extra-virgin olive oil for body, jalapeño chiles for heat, and cilantro for freshness (see Basics, p. 275), but even that formula is flexible as long as the acid and spice are present. Then I experiment with textures. Those fishermen may never have added basil cream or crisp Spanish migas to their simple fish dish, but the flavors make sense within the ceviche tradition.

My idea for this dish began with the contrasting flavors of Spanish olives and serrano ham. The flavors lent themselves to an escabeche, a traditional Spanish marinade. Crisp migas, which I always eat for breakfast when traveling in Spain, adds the crunch to this ceviche.

serves 4

tuna toro
with migas and
serrano-verdial escabeche

3/4 pound tuna toro

* 3/4 cup serrano-verdial escabeche

* 2 tablespoons migas

1 ounce dried serrano ham, zested (see Basics, p. 276)

Sea salt, to taste

Extra-virgin olive oil, to taste

*

serrano-verdial escabeche

Yields 3/4 cup

1/4 cup brunoised serrano ham

1/4 cup green Spanish olives, diced

1 tablespoon diced piquillo chiles (see
    Sources and Substitutions)

1/2 shallot, brunoised

2 tablespoons white wine vinegar

3 tablespoons extra-virgin olive oil

1 1/2 teaspoons finely chopped flat-leaf
    parsley

1/2 teaspoon granulated sugar

Kosher salt, to taste

• In a bowl, combine all ingredients.

*

migas

Yields 1/2 cup

1/2 day-old traditional French baguette

1 clove garlic

1/4 teaspoon kosher salt

1 ounce serrano ham fat (see Basics, p. 277)

1 teaspoon smoked paprika (see Sources
    and Substitutions)

• Remove crust from baguette and dice
bread into small pieces. In a sauté pan,
combine garlic, salt, and ham fat. Warm
over medium-high heat. Add bread and toss
until coated. Lower heat to medium and
toast until slightly colored and crisp.
Sprinkle with smoked paprika. Discard
garlic. Drain. Migas can be stored at room
temperature in a dry area for up to 1
week.

putting it all together

• Dice tuna toro. Toss tuna with escabeche
and divide between four rocks glasses.
Garnish with migas, dried serrano ham
zest, and sea salt. Drizzle with olive oil.
Serve with cocktail forks.

You'll find octopus and calamari on tapas menus all over Spain, usually served lightly charred a la plancha—on a flat-top grill. In this recipe, I've added traditional Spanish ingredients such as saffron and squid ink. The twist? The ingredients are combined simply, in a South American ceviche mixto style.

serves 4

octopus and calamari with saffron-shellfish sauce and squid ink reduction

2 ounces smoked bacon, cut into lardons

* 1/2 cup saffron-shellfish sauce

* 1/2 pound marinated octopus

* 1/2 pound marinated calamari

1 blood orange, segmented

* 1/2 cup squid ink reduction

*

saffron-shellfish sauce

Yields 1/2 cup

1/4 pound shrimp shells

1 1/2 teaspoons vegetable oil

1/2 shallot, brunoised

1/2 carrot, chopped

1 clove garlic, minced

1 tablespoon vegetable oil

1/2 cup clam juice

1 teaspoon saffron

1/4 cup heavy cream

3 tablespoons lemon juice

1 teaspoon kosher salt

• Preheat oven to 400°F. Toss shrimp shells
with oil, place on a cookie sheet in a single
layer, and roast 10 minutes.

• In a saucepan over low heat, sweat
shallots, carrots, and garlic in vegetable oil
until shallots are translucent. Add roasted
shrimp shells and clam juice, and simmer 5
minutes. Add saffron and cream and bring
back to a simmer. Add lemon juice and salt.
Puree with an immersion blender, and
strain through a fine-mesh strainer.

*

marinated octopus

Yields 1/2 pound

3 lemons, halved

1/2 cup pickling spice

1/2 cup kosher salt

2 tablespoons red pepper flakes

16 cups water

1 Spanish octopus (2 to 3 pounds)

4 wine corks

1/2 cup standard ceviche marinade (see
    Basics, p. 275)

• In a saucepan over high heat, bring
lemons, pickling spice, salt, red pepper
flakes, and water to a boil. Add octopus
and wine corks and cook until octopus is
tender, about 60 minutes. Remove octopus
and refrigerate to cool. Discard excess
liquid. Cut 1/2 pound of the octopus into
coins. (Remaining octopus can be frozen
for up to 2 weeks.) Marinate octopus coins
in ceviche marinade for at least 10
minutes. Remove from marinade.

*

marinated calamari

Yields 1/2 pound

4 cups vegetable stock (see Basics, p. 270)

1/2 pound calamari

1/4 cup standard ceviche marinade (see
    Basics, p. 275)

• Bring vegetable stock to a boil, blanch
calamari for 1 minute, and cool. Cut
calamari into rings and marinate in ceviche
marinade for 30 seconds. Remove calamari
from marinade.

*

squid ink reduction

Yields 1/2 cup

1/2 cup onion confit (see Basics, p. 272)

1/4 cup clam juice

1 tablespoon squid ink (see Sources and
    Substitutions)

Kosher salt, to taste

• Puree onion confit with clam juice in a
blender for 2 minutes. Add squid ink and
puree until mixture is completely black.
Place puree in a saucepan. Cook over
medium heat until reduced to 1/2 cup.
Season with salt and pass through a
chinois. Allow to cool.

putting it all together

• In a skillet over medium heat, cook bacon
until crisp. On a serving plate pour an
abstract puddle of the saffron-shellfish
sauce. Randomly place the octopus,
calamari, blood orange segments, and
bacon lardons on the plate. Using a squeeze
bottle, dot the saffron sauce with the
squid ink sauce.

I grew up with tomato-y shrimp ceviche, a staple served by the beach shacks in Salinas, Ecuador. We had it for breakfast or as an anytime snack. This recipe, my reinterpretation of that vivid memory, perfectly balances creamy avocado slices with chile-spiked popcorn, but the dish hinges on the tenderness of the prawns. Texture is key.

serves 4

spot prawns
with ecuadorian ceviche sauce
and spicy popcorn

12 poached spot prawns (see Basics, p. 277)

* 2 cups Ecuadorian ceviche sauce

1 tablespoon chopped cilantro

2 scallions, sliced

1/4 red onion, brunoised

1 avocado, sliced

Sea salt, to taste

Extra-virgin olive oil, to taste

* 2 cups spicy popcorn

*

spicy popcorn

Yields 2 cups

1 1/2 tablespoons cayenne pepper

1 tablespoon kosher salt

2 teaspoons smoked paprika (see Sources
and Substitutions)

1 teaspoon chile de arbol powder (see
Sources and Substitutions)

1 teaspoon granulated sugar

2 cups popped gourmet popcorn

• In a bowl, combine spices and sugar; mix
together thoroughly. Add popcorn to the
bowl and toss until completely coated.

putting it all together

• Marinate prawns in Ecuadorian ceviche
sauce for 10 to 15 minutes. Remove prawns
from sauce. Pour Ecuadorian ceviche sauce
into a shallow bowl. Garnish sauce with
cilantro, scallions, and red onion. Arrange
prawns around the rim of the bowl and lay
a slice of avocado over each one. Season
prawns and avocado with sea salt and
extra-virgin olive oil. Line a rocks glass with
a piece of parchment paper and fill with
spicy popcorn. Serve with ceviche.

*

ecuadorian ceviche sauce

Yields 2 cups

1 beefsteak tomato, cored

1 Spanish onion, quartered

1 jalapeño chile, seeded

1/2 red bell pepper, seeded

1/2 green bell pepper, seeded

Extra-virgin olive oil, as needed

1/4 cup lime juice

1/2 cup ketchup

1 cup orange juice

Tabasco sauce, to taste

• Coat all vegetables lightly in olive oil and
grill or cook under a broiler for 10 minutes
until charred. Remove from grill. In a food
processor, puree grilled vegetables and
remaining ingredients until smooth. Taste
and adjust seasoning as needed.

This is a totally American take on ceviche, inspired by well-known chef Thomas Keller, who owns French Laundry in California's wine country. He created the light, flavorful tomato water which I've used here in place of citrus juice. You can add any type of oyster, but I like small, briny ones from the West Coast best.

serves 4

kumamoto oysters
with tomato water
and cucumber gelée

12 Kumamoto oysters

* 12 shots cucumber gelée

* 1 cup tomato water

1 red jalapeño chile, brunoised fine

2 tablespoons small-diced baby fennel

1 teaspoon sea salt

12 fennel fronds

✳

cucumber gelée

Yields 12 shots

1 cup baby spinach

2 sheets gelatin

3 English cucumbers

1 teaspoon kosher salt

• In a pot of boiling water, blanch spinach for 1 minute. Shock spinach in cold water. Bloom gelatin in ice water. Squeeze out excess water. Peel cucumbers and slice in half lengthwise. Scoop out and discard seeds, reserving the cucumber flesh. Place the cucumbers in a vegetable juicer. (Juicer should extract 2 cups liquid.) In a saucepan over low heat, bring 1/4 cup cucumber juice to a simmer. Add gelatin to dissolve.

• In a blender, combine spinach, gelatin mixture and remaining cucumber juice. Season with salt. Pour 1/4 inch liquid into each of 12 shot glasses and refrigerate to set gelatin, about 1 hour.

✳

tomato water

Yields 1 cup

10 plum tomatoes

1 1/2 tablespoons sherry vinegar

2 tablespoons extra-virgin olive oil

2 tablespoons kosher salt

• Trim tops off and quarter tomatoes. Combine half of each ingredient in a food processor and puree for 30 seconds. Pour puree into a chinois and press out as much liquid as possible, reserving liquid; discard solids. Repeat with remaining ingredients. Strain liquid through a cheesecloth, and then strain through a coffee filter.

putting it all together

• Place one oyster into each cucumber gelée–filled shot glass. Divide tomato water, jalapeños, fennel, and salt among the 12 glasses. Garnish each with a fennel frond. Serve with demitasse spoons.

This dish breaks all the "rules" of ceviche. For one, the duck is cooked before it is added—slow roasted for hours, in fact. But it is a favorite in Peru, where it's served cold, mixto style with plenty of flavorful orange marinade and a sweet potato garnish.

serves 4

duck confit
with orange duck jus,
duck chicharrones, and foie gras

1 sweet potato, peeled and diced small

2 confit duck legs (see Basics, p. 276)

* 1/2 cup orange duck jus

2 tablespoons lime juice

1/2 cup julienned red onion

2 tablespoons cilantro chiffonade

1/4 pound foie gras torchon (see Basics, p. 276)

1 tablespoon turbinado sugar

* 8 pieces duck chicharrones

*

orange duck jus

Yields 2 cups

2 duck carcasses

2 carrots, diced

5 cloves garlic, chopped

2 cups diced Spanish onions

1/2 cup tomato paste

1/2 cup rocoto chile paste (see Basics, p. 271)

1/2 teaspoon red pepper flakes

1 cup sherry

2 cups orange juice

2 gallons water

• Preheat oven to 400°F. In a large roasting pan, spread carcasses in one layer. Roast carcasses until they take on a dark brown color, about 45 minutes. Remove from oven. To the same roasting pan add carrots, garlic, and onions. Place the pan on the stovetop and cook over medium heat. Once the vegetables have cooked down and the pan is clean, add tomato paste, chile paste, and red pepper flakes. Cook 5 minutes, stirring constantly. Add sherry and orange juice to deglaze the pan and simmer for 15 minutes.

• Place vegetables, carcasses, and liquid in a stockpot. Fill the pot with water. Bring mixture to a boil then reduce heat to a light simmer. Cook 2 hours.

• Strain stock. Return liquid to stockpot. Over high heat, reduce liquid to 2 cups. Orange duck jus can be refrigerated for up to 1 week or frozen for up to 1 month.

*

duck chicharrones

Yields 8 pieces

1 Moulard duck breast

• Preheat oven to its lowest setting. Remove skin from duck breast. Reserve duck breast for another use. Cut skin widthwise into four 1/2-inch strips. Cut each strip into 2 triangles and lay out on a nonstick ovenproof surface such as a Silpat. Cook skin until crisp, about 8 hours.

putting it all together

• Bring a pot of water to a boil. Blanch sweet potato for 2 minutes. Shock in cold water.

• Shred the duck meat and combine with orange duck jus, lime juice, sweet potato, red onion, and cilantro. Divide mixture among 4 rocks glasses, filling them about half full. Place the glasses in the refrigerator for 1 hour to set. Slice the torchon into four 1/4-inch-thick slices. Sprinkle with sugar and, using a blowtorch, brûlée the torchon. (If you don't have a blowtorch, just omit the sugar and this step.) Top each glass of confit with a slice of torchon and 2 pieces duck chicharrones.

I learned a lot about ceviche from chef Douglas Rodriguez, with whom I worked at Chicama and Pipa in New York and Alma de Cuba in Philadelphia. This recipe was inspired by concha negra, a type of black clam ceviche found on the coast of Ecuador.

serves 4

middleneck clams mixto
with salsa verde
and toasted corn nuts

1 shallot, sliced

1 tablespoon extra-virgin olive oil

20 middleneck clams

1 cup white wine

1 red jalapeño chile, brunoised

3 scallions, sliced thin

* 1/2 cup salsa verde

4 limes, zested and juiced

2 tablespoons cilantro chiffonade

10 chives, minced

Kosher salt, to taste

Granulated sugar, to taste

1 ounce dried serrano ham, zested (see Basics, p. 276)

* 1/4 cup toasted corn nuts

*

salsa verde

Yields 1/2 cup

1/4 cup basil leaves

1/4 cup cilantro leaves

1/4 cup flat-leaf parsley leaves

1/2 cup baby spinach

1/2 jalapeño chile, seeded and chopped

2 tablespoons clam juice

1 clove garlic

1 1/2 tablespoons extra-virgin olive oil

1 1/2 tablespoons vegetable oil

1/2 teaspoon kosher salt

• Bring a pot of water to a boil. Blanch basil for 10 seconds, shock in ice water; blanch cilantro and parsley separately, 30 seconds each, and shock in ice water; blanch baby spinach for 15 seconds, shock in ice water. Combine all ingredients in a blender and puree until mixture is combined, but not completely smooth. Season with salt.

*

toasted corn nuts

Yields 1/4 cup

1/4 cup corn nuts

1 teaspoon unsalted butter

1/2 teaspoon kosher salt

• In a sauté pan over low heat, gently toast corn nuts until slightly browned. Add butter and toss until melted. Season with salt, and drain.

putting it all together

• In a sauté pan over medium heat, sauté shallots in olive oil 2 minutes. Add clams and white wine. Cover and steam until clams open. Remove clams from shells and refrigerate until cool. Reserve shells. In a bowl, combine clams, jalapeño, and scallions. Add salsa verde to coat ingredients. Add lime zest and juice, cilantro, and chives. Season with salt and sugar.

• On a serving plate, arrange clamshells, and place a clam back into each shell. Garnish each clam with dried serrano ham zest. Serve with a small dish of toasted corn nuts

The Yucatán Peninsula is fertile ground for oranges and habanero chiles. These two ingredients are the basis of the classic xnipec sauce, which I use here as a ceviche marinade. One warning: Mexican ceviche is hotter than most versions of the dish.

serves 4

swordfish xnipec with pickled habanero chiles and candied orange zest

1/2 pound swordfish

* 1/4 cup habanero-orange sauce

4 teaspoons small-diced red onion

4 teaspoons cilantro chiffonade

4 teaspoons fine-julienned radish

3 scallions, sliced thin

8 orange segments

* 8 rings pickled habanero chiles

* 8 strips candied orange zest

*

habanero-orange sauce

Yields 1/2 cup

1 cup chopped Spanish onion

1 clove garlic, chopped

1 habanero chile, seeded and chopped

1/2 tablespoon vegetable oil

1 cup orange juice

1/2 cup apple cider vinegar

1 teaspoon red pepper flakes

1 tablespoon glucose syrup (see Sources
    and Substitutions)

1 tablespoon corn syrup

• In a large saucepan over low heat, sweat onion, garlic, and habaneros in vegetable oil for 10 minutes until onions are translucent. Add orange juice, vinegar, and red pepper flakes. Over high heat, reduce mixture by half. Strain mixture through a chinois and whisk in glucose syrup and corn syrup. Cook over medium-low heat for 20 minutes until slightly thicker than nappé.

*

pickled habanero chiles

Yields 8 rings

1 habanero chile, seeded and sliced into
    8 rings

1/4 shallot, julienned

1 bay leaf

1/4 teaspoon dried oregano

1/4 teaspoon dried thyme

1/4 cup orange juice

1/4 cup white wine vinegar

1 1/2 teaspoons granulated sugar

1 1/2 teaspoons kosher salt

• Combine all ingredients in a nonreactive container and refrigerate for at least 30 minutes. Pickled habaneros can be refrigerated for up to 2 weeks.

*

candied orange zest

Yields about 20 strips

1 navel orange

1/2 cup granulated sugar

1/2 cup water

• Peel orange, trim peels of all white pith, and finely julienne peels. In a small saucepan over medium heat, combine 1/4 cup sugar and 1/4 cup water and bring to a simmer. Add peels and blanch for 1 minute. Remove and allow to cool for 2 minutes. Discard blanching liquid. Repeat process, blanching peels a second time with remaining sugar and water. Store candied orange zest at room temperature in a dry area for up to 1 week.

putting it all together

• Slice swordfish into 1/8-inch-thick pieces. Arrange on 4 chilled plates. Dress each plate with habanero-orange sauce, red onion, cilantro, radish, scallions, 2 orange segments, 2 slices pickled habanero, and 2 strips candied orange zest.

Red snapper a la Veracruzana is a Mexican dinner staple. But one taste of the tomato-based Veracruzana sauce convinced me that the traditional dish could be transformed into a tasty ceviche similar to the ones I remember from my time in Ecuador. In this recipe, the Veracruzana sauce is a chilled salsa-like marinade for the red snapper.

serves 4

red snapper a la veracruzana with mini tostadas and avocado pearls

1/2 pound red snapper, cut into 16 cubes

1 1/3 cups standard ceviche marinade (see Basics, p. 275)

4 cups vegetable oil, for frying

2 tablespoons capers, drained

1 cup quartered cherry tomatoes

2 shallots, brunoised

1/2 cup Manzanilla olives, julienned

1/4 cup pickled jalapeño chile rings (see Basics, p. 273)

1/4 cup flat-leaf parsley chiffonade

2 tablespoons extra-virgin olive oil

* 1 cup Veracruzana sauce

16 mini tostadas (see Basics, p. 278)

1 avocado, cut into pearls using a tiny melon baller

*

veracruzana sauce

Yields 1 cup

1/2 cup chopped Spanish onion

1 clove garlic, chopped

1 1/2 teaspoons vegetable oil

1 1/2 plum tomatoes, chopped

2/3 cup clam juice

1/4 cup tomato juice

1/8 teaspoon dried marjoram

1/8 teaspoon dried thyme

1/2 dried bay leaf

1/8 stick canela (see Sources and
   Substitutions)

1 clove

1/8 teaspoon black peppercorns

1 1/2 teaspoons extra-virgin olive oil

1/2 teaspoon kosher salt

• In a saucepan over low heat, sweat onions
and garlic in vegetable oil until translucent.
Add tomatoes and cook over medium heat
for 15 minutes. Add clam and tomato juices.
Wrap marjoram, thyme, bay leaf, canela,
clove, and peppercorns in cheesecloth and
add to tomato mixture. Bring mixture to a
boil; reduce heat and simmer for 30
minutes. Remove herbs and spices. In a
blender, puree sauce, slowly adding olive oil
until emulsified. Season with salt. Strain
through a chinois. Veracruzana sauce can
be refrigerated for up to 2 days.

putting it all together

• Marinate snapper in standard ceviche
marinade for 2 to 5 minutes. Remove
snapper from marinade. In a fryer or deep,
heavy-bottomed 4-quart pan, heat
vegetable oil to 400°F. Add capers and fry
until crispy, about 30 seconds. Lay out on
paper towel to drain.

• In a bowl combine tomatoes, shallots,
olives, pickled jalapeños, parsley, and olive
oil, to make a fresh salsa.

• Divide Veracruzana sauce among 4 plates.
Arrange fresh salsa randomly in the
Veracruzana sauce. Add 4 cubes of snapper
to each plate. Garnish with tostadas,
avocado pearls, and fried capers.

Salmon is a common ceviche ingredient in Chile, where you'll find it garnished with orange, mint, and mustard. Whenever wild salmon is plentiful on the west coast of North America, I get the urge to make this classic dish. Ivory king salmon, lighter in color and taste than most varieties, is my top choice.

serves 4

ivory king salmon with mustard crème fraîche, mint, and orange vinaigrette

* 1/2 cup orange vinaigrette

  1/2 pound ivory king salmon, diced medium

  2 navel oranges, zested and segmented

* 1/4 cup mustard crème fraîche

  2 tablespoons mustard oil (see Basics, p. 267)

  3 tablespoons garlic chips (see Basics, p. 271)

  16 mint leaves

*

orange vinaigrette

Yields 3/4 cup

1 shallot, minced fine

2 tablespoons orange juice

2 tablespoons lime juice

1 teaspoon honey

1/4 cup mustard oil (see Basics, p. 267)

2 tablespoons mint chiffonade

Kosher salt, to taste

• In a bowl, combine shallots, orange juice, lime juice, and honey. While whisking, slowly add mustard oil until emulsified. Add mint chiffonade. Season with salt. Vinaigrette can be refrigerated for up to 1 week.

*

mustard crème fraîche

Yields 1/4 cup

1 1/2 tablespoons crème fraîche

1/2 tablespoon Dijon mustard

1/2 teaspoon whole-grain mustard

1/4 teaspoon kosher salt

• In a bowl, combine all ingredients.

putting it all together

• Pour orange vinaigrette into a serving bowl. Add salmon and orange segments. Marinate 5 to 10 minutes. Place a small dot of mustard crème fraîche on top of each piece of salmon. Drizzle mustard oil around each dot and top with a garlic chip. Sprinkle orange zest over plate. Garnish with mint leaves.

NOTE: photo on p. 47

As a chef, I'm always looking for vegetarian twists on traditional meat or fish dishes. This ceviche borrows its flavors from the Spanish pantry. Oil-poached artichokes, roasted tomatoes, marcona almonds, and smoked paprika create the same balance of flavor and texture common in fish-based South American ceviches.

serves 4

artichoke confit
with roasted tomato puree
and smoked marcona almonds

4 confit artichokes (see Basics, p. 271)

* 1/2 cup roasted tomato puree

2 shallots, brunoised

1/2 cup black olives, julienned very fine

1/2 cup piquillo chiles, brunoised (see Sources and Substitutions)

2 tablespoons smoked paprika oil (see Basics, p. 268)

3 tablespoons extra-virgin olive oil

* 2 tablespoons smoked marcona almonds

*

smoked marcona almonds

Yields 1/4 cup

1/2 cup almonds
4 cups wood chips

• If you have a smoker, place almonds on a sheet pan and place in the smoker for 10 minutes. If not, take a deep, flameproof pan and layer the bottom with wood chips that have been soaked in water overnight. On top of that, place a perforated pan and layer it with the almonds and place a cover over the almonds. Then place the pan over a high flame until wood chips start smoking hard. Turn the flame to medium and smoke for 8 minutes.

• Allow almonds to cool. Once they're completely cool, grind almonds in a food processor until crushed. Smoked almonds can be stored at room temperature in a dry area for up to 1 week.

*

roasted tomato puree

Yields 1/2 cup

1 1/2 plum tomatoes, halved lengthwise
1 tablespoon extra-virgin olive oil
1/2 teaspoon kosher salt
2 teaspoons thyme leaves
2 cloves roasted garlic (see Basics, p. 267)
1/4 teaspoon red pepper flakes
1 tablespoon sherry vinegar

• Preheat oven to 275°F. Lightly coat tomatoes in 1 teaspoon olive oil and sprinkle with salt. Arrange tomatoes in a single layer on a sheet pan with a rack. Roast for 45 minutes.

• In a blender, combine roasted tomatoes, thyme, roasted garlic, red pepper flakes, and vinegar and puree. Strain through a chinois, place back into blender and puree while adding remaining olive oil, until emulsified. Taste and adjust seasoning.

putting it all together

• Slice each artichoke in half vertically. Place a dollop of roasted tomato puree on each of 4 plates and stand one artichoke half in puree. Slice remaining artichokes very thin and toss with shallots, black olives, piquillo chiles, smoked paprika oil, and olive oil. Layer the artichoke slices onto each plate then top with the garnish mixture. Sprinkle plate with crushed almonds.

NOTE: photo on p. 46

the tradition of tiradito

If ceviche is the king of Peruvian cuisine, tiradito is its

prince, a new approach to an old tradition—which is

exactly how I like to think about cooking. • Tiradito

isn't that different from ceviche. Most tiradito recipes call

for fresh raw fish and just a few condiments and garnishes. But the

fish in tiradito is sliced thinly, not diced as it is in ceviche. The

technique became popular in the early 20th century. (Should we

thank the Japanese population that came to Peru with the tradition of carefully sliced sushi, or the fisherman of the northern coast of Peru, who carried long knives best suited to slicing their catch into long, thin strips?) And it is still evolving.   This modern approach to preparing raw fish sparks my imagination. The basics are familiar: raw fish dressed with an acid, often citrus; chiles, such as ají amarillo or jalapeño; and crisp garnishes that add texture to the dish. But why not use the same approach with ingredients like Kobe beef, balsamic vinegar, horseradish, and icy granité?

Ají amarillo is a Peruvian staple—and one of my favorite chiles, with its fruity flavor and intense heat. Here I've paired a fiery paste made from these yellow chiles with the sweetness of pineapple. The flavors put a South American tattoo on velvety hamachi, a fish usually associated with sushi.

serves 4

hamachi with pineapple–ají amarillo sauce, ginger-lime granité, and candied ginger

1/2 pound hamachi

* 2 tablespoons ginger-lime granité

* 8 pieces candied ginger, brunoised

* 1/4 cup pineapple–ají amarillo sauce

Sea salt, to taste

Extra-virgin olive oil, to taste

*

ginger-lime granité

Yields 1 cup

1/2 teaspoon invert sugar simple syrup (see
    Basics, p. 278)

1/4 cup granulated sugar

2/3 cup water

1 tablespoon diced fresh ginger

2 tablespoons lime juice

1 teaspoon grated lime zest

• In a saucepan over high heat, boil invert
sugar syrup, granulated sugar, water, and
ginger until sugar is dissolved, stirring
occasionally so that the sugar doesn't
burn. Remove from heat and allow mixture
to steep for 15 minutes. Stir in lime juice
and zest and strain mixture through a
chinois. Place in a plastic container, cover
and freeze for 2 hours. Granité can be
frozen for up to 1 week.

*

candied ginger

Yields 8 pieces

1 cup simple syrup (see Basics, p. 278)

8 (1/8-inch-thick) peeled fresh ginger coins

1/2 cup granulated sugar

1 teaspoon citric acid (see Sources and
    Substitutions)

• In a saucepan, combine simple syrup and
ginger. Cook over medium heat until ginger
becomes soft, about 1 hour. Strain ginger,
reserving syrup, refrigerated, for another
use. In a small bowl combine sugar and
citric acid. Toss ginger in bowl with sugar
mixture until completely coated. Lay out to
dry. Candied ginger can be refrigerated
for up to 1 week.

✱

pineapple–ají amarillo sauce

Yields 1 cup

1/4 cup plus 1 tablespoon minced Spanish
    onion

1 clove garlic, minced

1 tablespoon vegetable oil

1 cup chopped pineapple

1/2 tablespoon ají amarillo chile paste (see
    Basics, p. 271)

1/2 cup fish stock

1/4 cup pineapple juice

1/2 teaspoon saffron

1 tablespoon glucose syrup (see Sources
    and Substitutions)

1/4 teaspoon kosher salt

• In a saucepan over low heat, sweat onions
and garlic in vegetable oil until translucent.
Add chopped pineapple and cook, stirring
occasionally, 5 to 7 minutes, until pineapple
is very soft. Add ají amarillo chile paste,
stock, pineapple juice, and saffron and
bring to a boil. Reduce heat and simmer 15
minutes. Whisk glucose syrup into pineapple
mixture. Season with salt. Remove mixture
from heat, transfer to a nonreactive
container, and set in ice bath to chill.
Process until smooth in a blender. Sauce
can be refrigerated for up to 2 days.

putting it all together

• Cut hamachi into 1/8-inch-thick slices. Lay
slices on a serving plate, leaving a small
space between each piece. Scrape frozen
granité with a fork until fluffy. Place a
very small scoop of the granité between
each piece of hamachi. Garnish granité
with candied ginger. Sauce the plate by
placing a large dot of pineapple–ají
amarillo sauce on one side of the plate and
using the tip of a spoon to drag it out the
length of the plate. Top each piece of
hamachi with a sprinkle of sea salt and a
drizzle of olive oil.

The thin slices of fluke in this dish are reminiscent of crudo, the Italian way of preparing raw fish. Like ceviche, crudo was first popular among Italy's fishermen, who prepared the day's catch with whatever ingredients were on hand. Mediterranean flavors inspired this tiradito, and the garlic oil ties all the elements together.

serves 4

fluke with preserved lemon sauce and crispy lemon rings

4 cups vegetable oil (reserved from crispy lemon rings), for frying

4 sage leaves

1/2 pound fluke

* 1/2 cup preserved lemon sauce

* 4 crispy lemon rings

1/2 cup black olives, sliced

Sea salt, to taste

1/4 cup garlic oil, warmed (see Basics, p. 267)

*

preserved lemon sauce

Yields 1/2 cup

1/3 cup corn syrup

1/4 teaspoon cornstarch

1/4 cup water

1/2 teaspoon saffron

1 tablespoon thyme leaves

1 tablespoon lime juice

1 preserved lemon (see Basics, p. 278)

• In a saucepan over low heat, combine corn syrup, cornstarch, and water, and bring to a simmer. Add saffron, thyme, lime juice, and preserved lemon, and simmer an additional 10 minutes. In a food processor, puree all ingredients until smooth. Pass through a fine-mesh strainer.

*

crispy lemon rings

Yields about 8 rings

3 3/4 cups water

1 lemon, cut into 1/4-inch rings

1 cup granulated sugar

1 1/2 teaspoons red pepper flakes

4 cups vegetable oil, for frying

2 tablespoons all-purpose flour

1/4 cup cornstarch

1 teaspoon kosher salt, plus more to taste

1/2 cup lemon-lime soda

• In a saucepan over high heat, bring 1 1/4 cups water to a boil. Add lemon rings and blanch for 1 minute. Remove lemon rings and discard blanching liquid. Repeat process, blanching rings a second time in 1 1/4 cups fresh water. Remove lemon rings. Bring remaining water, sugar, and red pepper flakes to a boil. Blanch lemon rings for 5 to 7 minutes, until tender. Shock in ice water. Lay rings out to cool. When cool,

remove the inner part of the lemon, without cutting the peel. Reserve peel. Discard remainder of lemon.

• In a fryer or a deep, heavy-bottomed 4-quart pan, heat vegetable oil to 350°F. In a bowl, combine flour, cornstarch, salt, and soda. Mix thoroughly. Dip lemon rings in batter, allowing excess batter to drip off. Fry in oil until golden, about 2 minutes. Drain rings, and season with salt. Rings can be stored at room temperature in a dry area for up to 1 week.

putting it all together

• In a fryer or deep, heavy-bottomed 4-quart pan, heat oil reserved from crispy lemon rings to 375°F. Fry sage leaves for 10 seconds. Drain.

• Slice fluke into 1/8-inch-thick slices, and arrange like shingles on a serving plate. Leaving a little space next to the fluke, spread a line of preserved lemon sauce beside the fluke. Again leaving a little space, arrange lemon rings next to the preserved lemon sauce. On the sauce, alternate evenly spaced fried sage leaves with olive rings. Sprinkle fluke with a little sea salt and drizzle with garlic oil.

This is a truly global approach to Peruvian tiradito—
and an ode to my philosophy of using the best
ingredients available. My shopping list includes bluefin
tuna, a Japanese delicacy; aged balsamic vinegar
from Italy; aromatic Andalucian olive oil; and that
Latin American staple, jalapeño chiles. Very American
watermelon brings a sweetness to the dish.

serves 4

bluefin tuna
with spicy watermelon sauce
and black sesame seeds

1/2 pound bluefin tuna

8 slices yellow watermelon

* 3/4 cup spicy watermelon sauce

1/2 teaspoon 25-year-old balsamic vinegar

2 teaspoons toasted black sesame seeds

5 basil leaves, cut into a chiffonade

Sea salt, to taste

2 tablespoons Arbequina olive oil (see Sources and Substitutions)

*

spicy watermelon sauce

Yields 1 cup

1 red jalapeño chile, seeded

1/2 shallot, chopped

1/8 carrot, chopped

1/2 plum tomato, chopped

1 clove garlic, minced

2 tablespoons vegetable oil

1/4 cup glucose syrup (see Sources and
   Substitutions)

1 cup chopped seedless watermelon

2 teaspoons grenadine

• In a saucepan over low heat, sweat
jalapeños, shallots, carrots, tomatoes, and
garlic in vegetable oil until tender. Add
glucose syrup and cook over low heat for 5
minutes. In a food processor, puree mixture
until smooth. Add watermelon and
grenadine, and blend. Pass mixture through
a chinois, and chill. Sauce can be
refrigerated for up to 2 days.

putting it all together

• Slice tuna into 1/8-inch-thick slices. Cut
yellow watermelon the same way. Pour
spicy watermelon sauce onto a serving
plate. Dot with balsamic vinegar. Arrange
alternating shingles of tuna and watermelon
in a straight line on top of the sauce.
Sprinkle the plate with the sesame seeds,
and garnish the tuna with basil chiffonade
and sea salt. Drizzle with olive oil.

It would seem that you couldn't get much further from a Peruvian fisherman's snack than this haute dish. But for me, truffles and Meyer lemon don't obscure the essence of this recipe: This is a tiradito. The soul of the dish is there, most noticeably in the sweet sea scallops.

serves 4

sea scallops
with truffled lemon vinaigrette
and meyer lemon air

4 U/10 diver sea scallops, in shells

Sea salt, to taste

* 1/4 cup truffled lemon vinaigrette

1 black truffle, for shaving (see Sources and Substitutions)

1 lemon, zested

16 sprigs micro arugula

* 4 teaspoons Meyer lemon air

*

truffled lemon vinaigrette

Yields 10 tablespoons

1/2 shallot, brunoised

1 tablespoon chopped black truffle peels
(see Sources and Substitutions)

1/2 teaspoon chopped flat-leaf parsley

1/4 cup lemon juice

1 tablespoon black truffle oil (see Sources
and Substitutions)

1/4 cup extra-virgin olive oil

1/8 teaspoon granulated sugar

1/4 teaspoon kosher salt

• In a bowl, combine all ingredients. Check
seasoning and chill. Vinaigrette can be
refrigerated for up to 1 week.

*

meyer lemon air

Yields about 2 cups

3 Meyer lemons, zested and juiced

1/4 cup water

1 tablespoon granulated sugar

1/4 teaspoon soy lecithin (see Sources and
Substitutions)

• In a saucepan over low heat, combine
lemon juice and zest, water, and sugar.
When sugar has dissolved, add lecithin.
When lecithin has dissolved, remove from
heat and strain liquid though a fine mesh.
Buzz with a hand blender until foamy. Use
immediately.

putting it all together

• Open scallops and clean by removing the
pink roe and the beard with a scallop knife.
Slice each scallop into five thin circles.
Arrange scallop slices in shells and season
with salt. Spoon truffled lemon vinaigrette
over scallops. Top each scallop with 3
truffle shavings and lemon zest. Garnish
with arugula. Using a fork so that you don't
get any liquid, scoop lemon air onto each
scallop.

Here I've applied the logic of the tiradito to the classic American pairing of beef and horseradish. Just before serving, I add a traditional ceviche marinade to give a South American twist to the familiar flavors.

serves 4

kobe beef
with horseradish cream
and royal trumpet mushrooms

1/2 pound Kobe tenderloin (see Sources and Substitutions)

* 1/4 cup black pepper rub

2 tablespoons vegetable oil

2 royal trumpet mushrooms, sliced thin (see Sources and Substitutions)

2 tablespoons micro parsley

Sea salt, to taste

1 tablespoon black truffle oil (see Sources and Substitutions)

2 teaspoons standard ceviche marinade (see Basics, p. 275)

2 tablespoons garlic chips (see Basics, p. 271)

* 1/4 cup horseradish cream

1 lemon, zested

4 sprigs micro parsley

*

black pepper rub

Yields 1/4 cup

2 tablespoons black pepper

1 tablespoon kosher salt

1 tablespoon granulated sugar

• In a bowl, combine all ingredients.

*

horseradish cream

Yields 1/2 cup

1/4 cup horseradish

1/2 cup heavy cream

• In a saucepan, combine horseradish and cream and blend with a hand blender until thoroughly combined. Over medium heat, bring mixture to a boil, and then reduce to a rapid simmer. Cook to reduce to 1/2 cup, about 7 minutes, stirring frequently. Horseradish cream can be refrigerated for up to 1 week.

putting it all together

• Rub tenderloin with black pepper rub. In a sauté pan over high heat, sear tenderloin on all sides in 1 tablespoon vegetable oil, until rare. Cool tenderloin, and wrap in plastic. Put tenderloin in the freezer for 4 hours. Remove tenderloin and slice into about 16 thin pieces. Lay slices on parchment paper overlapping each piece by half.

• In a sauté pan over high heat, sear mushrooms on both sides in the remaining 1 tablespoon vegetable oil. In a bowl, combine mushrooms and parsley, and toss with salt and truffle oil.

• Layer tenderloin onto 4 plates, with slices slightly overlapping. Drizzle with ceviche marinade and top with mushrooms and garlic chips. Smear a line of horseradish cream next to the tenderloin and top with lemon zest and micro parsley.

The tiradito roots of this dish are not easy to find.
Hint: look at the marinade, the cut of the
mushrooms, and the contrasting textures. I make
this dish with my favorite types of mushrooms, but
any mushrooms you like will be delicious, too.

serves 4

forest mushrooms
with lemon-shallot marinade
and white asparagus

5 ounces chanterelle mushrooms

5 ounces royal trumpet mushrooms (see Sources and Substitutions)

5 ounces blue foot mushrooms (see Sources and Substitutions)

5 ounces crimini mushrooms

1/4 cup vegetable oil

2 tablespoons kosher salt

1 teaspoon black pepper

12 confit cherry tomatoes (see Basics, p. 272)

4 stalks white asparagus, bias cut into 1 1/2-inch lengths

* 3/4 cup lemon-shallot marinade

1/4 cup micro basil

1 teaspoon coarse sea salt

1 tablespoon Arbequina olive oil (see Sources and Substitutions)

*

lemon-shallot marinade

Yields 3/4 cup

2 lemons

2 shallots, minced

1 clove garlic, minced

1/3 cup extra-virgin olive oil

1 tablespoon black truffle oil (see Sources
   and Substitutions)

1 teaspoon kosher salt

• Zest one lemon and juice them both.
Combine zest, lemon juice and remaining
ingredients.

putting it all together

• Preheat oven to 350°F. Toss the
mushrooms with vegetable oil, salt, and
pepper. Lay mushrooms out on a sheet tray
and roast until tender, about 10 minutes.

• In a bowl, combine roasted mushrooms
with confit cherry tomatoes and
asparagus and toss with the lemon-shallot
marinade.

• Arrange mushroom mixture on a plate.
Garnish with the micro basil. Sprinkle sea
salt and Arbequina olive oil over the
mushrooms.

The central ingredient in this tiradito comes from the cool waters of Maine, but it was the balmy Caribbean—and its use of extremely hot chiles—that inspired me to create this combination. Habanero chiles and coconut milk provide the basic tiradito elements and give the dish a solid island identity.

serves 4

maine lobster with coconut-habanero sauce and lime sorbet

1/4 cup thinly sliced chives

1/4 cup small-diced red onion

* 1/2 cup coconut-habanero sauce

4 poached Maine lobsters (see Basics, p. 277)

* 1/4 cup lime sorbet

1 lime, zested

1 habanero chile, seeded and julienned

✳

coconut-habanero sauce

Yields 3/4 cup

1 shallot, chopped

1/4 habanero chile, seeded

1 clove garlic, chopped

1 tablespoon vegetable oil

1/4 cup clam juice

1 cup coconut milk

1/4 teaspoon kosher salt

• In a saucepan over low heat, sweat shallots, habanero, and garlic in vegetable oil until shallots are translucent. Add clam juice and bring to a boil. Reduce heat to a simmer. Add coconut milk and reduce mixture by half, about 10 minutes. Remove habanero and discard. In a food processor, puree coconut milk mixture until smooth. Season with salt. Strain through a chinois. Sauce can be refrigerated for up to 2 days.

✳

lime sorbet

Yields 1 cup

1/4 cup granulated sugar

1/4 cup water

1 1/3 tablespoons invert sugar (see Sources and Substitutions)

6 tablespoons plus 2 teaspoons lime juice

• In a saucepan over medium heat, bring sugar, water, and invert sugar to a boil. Stir in lime juice. Pour mixture into a nonreactive container and refrigerate until cool. Pour cooled mixture into an ice cream maker and follow manufacturer's instructions. Sorbet can be frozen for up to 1 week.

putting it all together

• In a bowl, combine chives, red onions, and coconut-habanero sauce. Divide the mixture evenly among 4 plates. Crack open the lobster claws and tails and remove the meat. Slice each tail into thin slices. Arrange the meat from one claw and one tail on each sauced plate. Garnish with a small scoop of lime sorbet and lime zest. Sprinkle with habanero.

entradas

appetizers

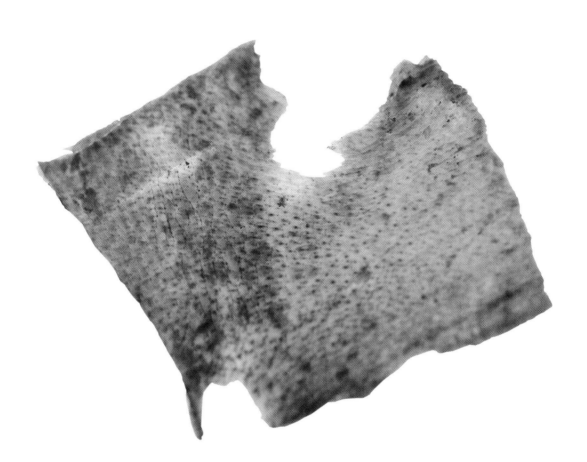

Americans don't have the same craving for octopus that Spanish diners do. That's probably because until recently it was difficult to find high-quality octopus in the United States. Here, I've taken the classic Old World pulpo gallego recipe and introduced some modern cooking techniques. But I still use a very classic method of tenderizing the octopus: boiling it with wine corks.

serves 4

octopus with yukon gold potato confit, lemon-garlic vinaigrette, and olive oil air

1/4 cup vegetable oil

* 3/4 pound marinated octopus

Kosher salt, to taste

12 slices confit Yukon Gold potato (see Basics, p. 272)

4 cloves garlic, minced

2 tablespoons lemon juice

* 1/4 cup lemon-garlic vinaigrette

* 1/4 cup olive oil air

2 teaspoons smoked paprika (see Sources and Substitutions)

＊

marinated octopus

Yields 3/4 to 1 pound

3 lemons, halved

1/2 cup pickling spice

1/2 cup kosher salt

2 tablespoons red pepper flakes

16 cups water

1 Spanish octopus (2 to 3 pounds)

4 wine corks

1/2 cup standard ceviche marinade (see
   Basics, p. 275)

• In a saucepan over high heat, bring lemons, pickling spice, salt, red pepper flakes, and water to a boil. Add octopus and wine corks and cook until octopus is tender, about 60 minutes. Remove octopus and refrigerate to cool. Discard liquid. Cut octopus into coins and marinate in ceviche marinade for at least 10 minutes. Remove from marinade. Octopus can be refrigerated for up to 2 days.

＊

lemon-garlic vinaigrette

Yields 6 tablespoons

2 cloves roasted garlic (see Basics, p. 267)

2 tablespoons lemon juice

1/4 cup extra-virgin olive oil

1/2 teaspoon kosher salt

• In a bowl, mash garlic. Mix in lemon juice and olive oil. Season with salt. Vinaigrette can be refrigerated for up to 2 days.

＊

olive oil air

Yields about 1 cup

1/2 cup vegetable stock, warmed (see
   Basics, p. 270)

1/8 teaspoon soy lecithin (see Sources and
   Substitutions)

1 1/2 tablespoons extra-virgin olive oil

1/2 teaspoon kosher salt

• In a cup, combine all ingredients and blend with a hand blender until a thick froth forms. Use immediately.

putting it all together

• In a cast-iron skillet over high heat, heat oil until almost smoking. Cut octopus into twelve 1-inch-long sections, and season with salt. Sear octopus and potato coins on all sides until crisp, about 1 minute per side. Remove from heat. Add garlic and lemon juice, tossing the pan continuously so garlic doesn't burn.

• Pour a pool of lemon-garlic vinaigrette onto a serving plate. Arrange potato coins in the vinaigrette, and place the pieces of octopus between the potato coins. Using a fork so that you don't get any liquid, scoop olive oil air onto each piece of octopus. Sprinkle with smoked paprika.

Any time, day or night, you'll find revuelto on the menu in Spain's tapas bars, especially in the Basque region. As an everyday meal, I like to mix the softly scrambled eggs with shrimp, mushrooms, or asparagus, but sometimes I can't resist dressing them up with lobster for an instantly impressive dish.

serves 2

eggs scrambled
with lobster, shellfish aïoli,
and cava cream

2 tablespoons unsalted butter

4 scallions, sliced into small rings

1/4 cup caramelized pearl onions, chopped (see Basics, p. 271)

1/4 cup roasted chanterelle mushrooms (see Basics, p. 273)

1/2 roasted plum tomato, cut in two (see Basics, p. 273)

3 ounces poached lobster meat, sliced (see Basics, p. 277)

2 large eggs

Kosher salt, to taste

1 tablespoon black truffle oil (see Sources and Substitutions)

* 1/4 cup cava cream

4 kumamoto oysters, shucked

2 tablespoons minced chives

* 2 tablespoons shellfish aïoli

2 toast points

1 teaspoon osetra caviar

*

cava cream

Yields 1/2 cup

1 shallot, chopped

1 clove garlic, chopped

1 tablespoon vegetable oil

1 cup cava or other sparkling wine

1 cup heavy cream

1/2 teaspoon lime juice

1/2 teaspoon kosher salt

• In a saucepan over low heat, sweat shallots and garlic in vegetable oil until translucent. Add cava and reduce to 1/2 cup. Add cream and reduce to 1/2 cup. Add lime juice and season with salt. Strain. Cava cream can be refrigerated for up to 1 week.

*

shellfish aïoli

Yields about 1/2 cup

1/2 cup white shrimp stock (see Basics, p. 270)

1 large egg yolk

1 clove garlic, zested

1 piquillo chile (see Sources and Substitutions)

1 tablespoon lemon juice

1/4 cup extra-virgin olive oil

1/4 teaspoon kosher salt

• In a saucepan over high heat, reduce shrimp stock to 2 tablespoons. In a food processor, combine all ingredients except oil and salt. Puree until smooth. While pureeing, slowly add olive oil, processing until emulsified. Season with salt. Aïoli can be refrigerated for up to 2 days.

putting it all together

• In a sauté pan over high heat, melt butter. Add scallions, caramelized onions, mushrooms, tomato, and lobster. Sauté mixture over medium heat for 1 minute. In a separate bowl, scramble eggs. Pour eggs into pan, season with salt, and stir with a rubber spatula continuously until egg is shirred.

• Place a 3-inch ring mold on each of two plates and divide egg mixture between the molds. Pack mixture down and remove mold. Drizzle with truffle oil.

• In a saucepan over high heat, reheat 1/4 cup cava cream. Add oysters and chives. Spread a line of cava cream next to molded egg mixture. Place oysters in the cream.

• Spread an even layer of shellfish aïoli on toast points; spread caviar over aïoli and use toast points to garnish plates.

Croquettes are everywhere in Spain—but, too often, they are doughy and heavy. So I went in search of a better recipe. The secret? While most Spanish croquettes call for a flour-and-water roux, this one calls for gelatin. The difference is amazing. These croquettes have a crisp exterior and a saucy, creamy interior. (NOTE: To make the espuma you'll need a whipped cream charger.)

serves 6

brandade croquettes and serrano ham croquettes with fresh tomato puree and cabrales espuma

2 cups all-purpose flour

10 large eggs

2 cups finely ground bread crumbs

* 12 brandade croquettes

* 12 serrano ham croquettes

8 cups vegetable oil, for frying

* 1 cup fresh tomato puree

1/2 ounce osetra caviar

* 3 tablespoons Cabrales espuma

brandade croquettes

12 croquettes

6 ounces bacalao, cut into large chunks
  (see Sources and Substitutions)

1 cup chopped Spanish onion

1 tablespoon extra-virgin olive oil

1/2 cup peeled and chopped Idaho potatoes

1 cup heavy cream

4 cups water

1 sprig rosemary

3 cloves roasted garlic (see Basics, p. 267)

3 sheets gelatin

Kosher salt, to taste

• Place bacalao in saucepan; fill pan with water. Over high heat, bring water to a boil. Strain off water and repeat process 3 times to desalinize fish.

• In a saucepan, combine onion and olive oil. Cook over low heat for 30 minutes, until onion is very tender. Strain onion mixture, reserving onions and oil separately.

• At the same time, in a separate saucepan, combine potato, heavy cream, 4 cups water, and rosemary. Over high heat, bring to a boil and then reduce to a simmer. (These steps must be done simultaneously so all mixtures will be hot when pureed.) Strain potato mixture, reserving potatoes and cream separately

• In a food processor, combine fish, onions, half of potatoes, and roasted garlic. Puree for about 30 seconds. Bloom gelatin in ice water. Squeeze excess water from bloomed gelatin sheets. To pureed mixture, add bloomed gelatin, reserved onion oil and cream from the potato mixture. Puree until creamy, but not completely smooth. Season with salt. Pour mixture onto sheet tray and cool.

• Roll dough into 2-tablespoon balls, placing on a tray lined with parchment. Put in the freezer to set, 1 hour. Brandade croquettes can be frozen for up to 1 week.

*

serrano ham croquettes

12 croquettes

3 ounces pork butt, diced small

1/4 tablespoon vegetable oil

1/2 cup small-diced Spanish onion

2 tablespoons small-diced red bell pepper

2 tablespoons unsalted butter

1 ounce serrano ham fat (see Basics, p. 277)

1/4 cup all-purpose flour

1 cup whole milk

1 sheet gelatin

1 ounce serrano ham butt, diced small

• In a braising pan, combine diced pork butt and vegetable oil. Over medium-low heat, render the pork until crisp. Add onion, peppers, butter, and ham fat. Cook over medium heat until peppers and onions are soft. Reduce heat to low and add flour. Mix thoroughly and cook 10 minutes, stirring several times. Add milk gradually, incorporating with a rubber spatula, as the mixture thickens and becomes smooth. Bloom gelatin in ice water. Squeeze excess water from bloomed gelatin sheets, and stir gelatin into mixture until dissolved. Turn off heat and add serrano ham. Mix thoroughly. Pour onto a sheet tray and cool.

• Roll into 2-tablespoon cylinders, place on a tray lined with parchment. Put in the freezer to set, 1 hour. Serrano ham croquettes can be frozen for up to 1 week.

*

Fresh tomato puree

Yields 1 cup

4 plum tomatoes, quartered

1 clove garlic

1 tablespoon sherry vinegar

2 tablespoons extra-virgin olive oil

1 teaspoon kosher salt

• In a food processor, puree tomatoes, garlic, vinegar, and oil. Season with salt. Strain through a chinois. Use immediately.

*

cabrales espuma

Yields about 1 cup

1/2 cup heavy cream

1 ounce Cabrales or other blue cheese

1/2 sheet gelatin

• In a saucepan over low heat, warm heavy cream. Whisk in cheese until melted. Bloom gelatin in ice water. Remove cream mixture from heat and whisk in bloomed gelatin. Cream mixture can be refrigerated for up to 2 days. When ready to use, fill a whipped cream charger halfway with the mixture and charge with 2 nitrous canisters. Place the charger in a warm place until use. (Do not charge more than 3 hours in advance.)

putting it all together

• To bread croquettes, arrange 3 large bowls. Place flour in first bowl. Whisk eggs in second bowl. Place bread crumbs in third bowl. Working with no more than 10 brandade or ham croquettes at a time, drop croquettes into flour, shaking bowl until croquettes are completely coated. Remove croquettes from flour, shaking off excess, and put into bowl with eggs. Shake bowl until croquettes are completely covered in egg. Remove croquettes from egg, shake off excess, and put into bowl with bread crumbs. Shake bowl until croquettes are evenly coated. Remove croquettes from bread crumbs, shake off excess and place on a tray lined with parchment paper. Refrigerate, uncovered. Breaded croquettes can be refrigerated for up to 3 days.

• In a fryer or deep, heavy-bottomed 4-quart pan, heat vegetable oil to 350°F. Drop croquettes into the fryer until golden brown, about 30 seconds. Place on paper towels to drain.

• Divide fresh tomato puree among 6 rocks glasses. Divide caviar among 3 of the glasses, and the Cabrales espuma among the other 3 glasses. Skewer brandade croquettes, 4 to a skewer, and balance on each of the three glasses with caviar. Skewer Serrano ham croquettes, 4 to a skewer, and balance on each of the 3 glasses with the Cabrales espuma.

I learned how to make gazpacho while I was working in Seville. In Spain, gazpacho is not the chunky, chilled tomato soup I was familiar with at home. Rather, it is smooth and well balanced. Many chefs drink it straight from a glass.

serves 4

heirloom tomato gazpacho with cucumber salad and yellow tomato chips

* 4 servings cucumber gelée

* 1 cup cucumber salad

* 4 cups heirloom tomato gazpacho

* 4 yellow tomato chips

*

cucumber gelée

Yields 4 servings

1 cup baby spinach

2 sheets gelatin

3 English cucumbers

1 teaspoon kosher salt

• In a pot of boiling water, blanch spinach for 1 minute. Shock spinach in cold water. Bloom gelatin in ice water. Squeeze out excess water. Peel cucumbers and slice in half lengthwise. Scoop out and discard seeds, reserving the cucumber flesh. Place the cucumbers in a vegetable juicer. (Juicer should extract 2 cups liquid.) In a saucepan over low heat, bring 1/4 cup cucumber juice to a simmer. Add gelatin to dissolve.

• In a blender, combine spinach, gelatin mixture and remaining cucumber juice. Season with salt. Pour 1/4 inch liquid into each of 4 rocks glasses and refrigerate to set, about 1 hour.

*

cucumber salad

Yields 1 cup

2/3 English cucumber, peeled and brunoised

1 1/3 shallots, brunoised

1 1/3 tomatillos, brunoised

1 1/2 teaspoons chopped flat-leaf parsley

2 teaspoons Meyer lemon juice

2 teaspoons extra-virgin olive oil

1 teaspoon kosher salt

• In a bowl, combine cucumber, shallots, tomatillos, and parsley. Toss with lemon juice, olive oil, and salt. Salad can be refrigerated for up to 24 hours.

*

heirloom tomato gazpacho

Yields 4 cups

4 large red heirloom tomatoes, cored

2/3 English cucumber, seeded

3 cloves garlic

1/3 cup sherry vinegar

3 tablespoons diced day-old baguette, crust removed

1/3 cup extra-virgin olive oil

2 tablespoons granulated sugar

1 teaspoon kosher salt

1/2 teaspoon black pepper

• Dip tomatoes into boiling water for 15 seconds then shock in ice water. Peel tomatoes.

• In a blender, combine tomatoes, cucumber, garlic, vinegar, and bread. Puree until smooth, slowly adding olive oil until emulsified. Season with sugar, salt, and pepper. Gazpacho can be refrigerated for up to 2 days.

*

yellow tomato chips

Yields about 10 chips

1 yellow beefsteak tomato, sliced paper-thin

• Preheat oven to 200°F. Lay tomatoes on a nonstick ovenproof surface, such as a Silpat, and place on sheet tray. Cover with another Silpat. Cook until tomatoes are completely dried, about 1 hour. Uncover and cool. Chips can be stored at room temperature in a dry area for up to 1 week.

putting it all together

• Remove cucumber gelée from the refrigerator and pack 1/4 cup cucumber salad into each glass. Fill each with 1 cup gazpacho. Top each with a tomato chip.

This soup surprised diners when I first served it at El Vez in Philadelphia. While it isn't a traditional Mexican dish, it does use common Mexican ingredients—with corn in the starring role.

serves 4

sweet corn soup with huitlacoche quesadillas and caviar crème fraîche

8 cups vegetable oil, for frying

* 8 huitlacoche quesadillas

* 1/4 cup caviar crème fraîche

12 popcorn shoots (see Sources and Substitutions)

* 4 cups sweet corn soup

*

huitlacoche quesadillas

Yields 8 quesadillas

3/4 cup masa harina (see Sources and
   Substitutions)

3/4 tablespoon lard

3/4 cup water

Kosher salt, to taste

1/2 cup huitlacoche filling (see following
   recipe)

• Knead masa harina, lard, water, and salt
together until a dough forms, cover with a
slightly damp cloth and store in the
refrigerator until ready to use.

• Divide dough into 8 balls. Line a tortilla
press with plastic wrap and press 1 ball
flat, or roll flat with a rolling pin into 3-
inch tortillas. Fill immediately with 1
tablespoon huitlacoche filling. Fold
quesadilla in half. Press the ends together
to seal. Cook immediately.

huitlacoche filling

Yields 1 cup

3/4 shallot, julienned

1 clove garlic, minced

1 1/2 teaspoons vegetable oil

1/2 cup thinly sliced crimini mushrooms

1 1/2 teaspoons huitlacoche (see Sources
   and Substitutions)

2 ounces Chihuahua cheese, grated

1 tablespoon finely chopped flat-leaf
   parsley

4 1/2 teaspoons chopped cilantro

1/2 lemon, zested

1 tablespoon black truffle oil (see Sources
   and Substitutions)

Kosher salt, to taste

• In a saucepan over low heat, sweat
shallots and garlic in vegetable oil until
translucent. Add mushrooms and
huitlacoche, and sauté over high heat.
Reduce heat to low and stir in Chihuahua
cheese. Once the cheese has melted,
remove pan from heat. Fold in parsley,
cilantro, lemon zest, and truffle oil. Season
with salt and chill. Huitlacoche filling can
be refrigerated for up to 2 days.

✳

caviar crème fraîche

Yields 1/4 cup

1 ounce osetra caviar

1/4 cup crème fraîche

Pinch kosher salt

• In a bowl, combine caviar, crème fraîche, and salt. Mix gently. Allow to chill in refrigerator for 1 hour before serving.

✳

sweet corn soup

Yields 4 cups

2 cups chopped Spanish onion

3 cloves garlic

1 tablespoon unsalted butter

1 teaspoon saffron

3 ears corn, kernels removed from cob

2 teaspoons kosher salt

4 cups corn stock (see Basics, p. 269)

2 cups heavy cream

1 tablespoon granulated sugar

• In a saucepan over low heat, sweat onions and garlic in butter until translucent. Add saffron and sweat until bright yellow. Add corn kernels and season with salt. Sauté corn until soft. Add corn stock and bring mixture to a boil. Reduce to a simmer and cook for 20 minutes. Add heavy cream and bring to a boil over high heat once again. Reduce heat and simmer for 10 minutes. Puree soup in a blender and strain through a chinois. Season with sugar.

putting it all together

• In a fryer or deep, heavy-bottomed 4-quart pan, heat vegetable oil to 350°F. Fry quesadillas until golden brown.

• Shape crème fraîche into 4 small quenelles and place one in the bottom of each of 4 bowls. Set 2 quesadillas on each quenelle. Garnish with popcorn shoots. Pour sweet corn soup into a teapot and pour the soup into the bowls tableside.

You can think of this incredibly versatile dish as a Spanish frittata. Start with the basics—eggs, onions, and potatoes—and then add your favorite flavors. (Shrimp and chorizo is another one of my top combinations.)

serves 4

chanterelle-and-artichoke tortillas españolas with romesco aïoli

* 4 chanterelle-and-artichoke tortillas Españolas

* 4 teaspoons romesco aïoli

  1 tablespoon micro parsley

*

chanterelle-and-artichoke

tortillas españolas

Yields 4 tortillas Españolas

3 cups vegetable oil, for blanching, plus
 2 tablespoons

1 large Idaho potato, peeled and diced small

2 cups small-diced Spanish onion

2 ounces roasted chanterelle mushrooms
 (see Basics, p. 273)

4 confit artichokes, chopped (see Basics,
 p. 271)

5 large eggs, beaten

2 teaspoons kosher salt

1/4 teaspoon black pepper

8 teaspoons extra-virgin olive oil

Nonstick cooking spray

• Preheat oven to 300°F. In a fryer or a
deep, heavy-bottomed pan, heat 3 cups
vegetable oil to 250°F. Blanch potatoes in
oil until crisp. Lay on a tray to cool.

• In a saucepan over low heat, sweat onion
in remaining vegetable oil until translucent.
Cool.

• In a bowl, combine potato, onion,
mushrooms, artichokes, and eggs. Season
with salt and pepper. In a 3-inch nonstick
pan over low heat, heat 2 teaspoons olive
oil. Fill pan with 1 cup egg mixture. Cook
over low heat until the bottom layer is
cooked but there is no color, 2 to 3
minutes. Invert a second pan coated with
nonstick cooking spray on top of the first.

Flip the egg mixture into the second pan.
Cook the other side of the tortilla over low
heat to set, 2 to 3 minutes. Remove tortilla
from pan and set on sheet tray. Repeat
cooking process for remaining egg mixture
to make 4 tortillas. Cover tortillas tightly
with aluminum foil and bake until tortillas
are firm, about 12 minutes. Allow to rest
for 2 minutes before cutting.

*

romesco aïoli

Yields 1/2 cup

1/3 cup standard romesco sauce (see
 Basics, p. 275)

1/4 cup standard aïoli (see Basics, p. 275)

1/8 teaspoon kosher salt

• In a bowl, fold romesco sauce into aïoli.
Season with salt. Aïoli can be refrigerated
for up to 2 days; refresh with lemon juice
and sherry vinegar before using.

putting it all together

• Cut tortillas in half and place 2 halves
onto each of 4 plates. In between halves
place 1 teaspoon of the romesco aïoli and
top each wedge with a few sprigs of micro
parsley.

This is one Spanish dish that always surprises American diners: squid served in its own black ink. I use a classic Basque recipe to prepare the squid, and then serve it with a risotto-style rice and a rich crab cream. The crab enhances the briny flavor of the squid—and it makes people who are unfamiliar with the dish more likely to try it.

serves 4

baby squid
with crab bomba rice
and squid ink sauce

3/4 pound chipirones (baby squid; see Sources and Substitutions)

2 tablespoons vegetable oil

1/4 cup clam juice

* 1/2 cup squid ink sauce

2 tablespoons unsalted butter

* 1 1/4 cup cooked bomba rice

* 1/2 cup crab cream

3 ounces jumbo lump crabmeat

1/4 cup scallion greens, cut lengthwise

1 tablespoon parsley oil (see Basics, p. 267)

*

bomba rice

Yields 1 1/4 cups

1 cup small-diced Spanish onion

1 clove garlic, minced

1 tablespoon vegetable oil

1/2 cup uncooked bomba rice (see Sources
    and Substitutions)

1 1/4 cups clam juice

1/4 teaspoon kosher salt

• Preheat oven to 325°F. In an ovenproof
saucepan over low heat, sweat onions and
garlic in vegetable oil until onions are
translucent. Add rice and stir to coat. Add
clam juice and season with salt. Bring
mixture to a simmer over medium heat.
Cover tightly and bake for 18 minutes. Pour
rice onto a tray and fluff with a fork.
Cooked rice can be refrigerated for up to
24 hours.

*

squid ink sauce

Yields 1/2 cup

1/4 cup onion confit (see Basics, p. 272)

2 cloves roasted garlic (see Basics, p. 273)

1 tablespoon vegetable oil

1 tablespoon squid ink (see Sources and
    Substitutions)

1 cup clam juice

• In a saucepan over low heat, sweat onion
confit and roasted garlic in vegetable oil
until translucent. Stir in squid ink and clam
juice. Bring mixture to a boil and then
reduce to a simmer. Cook for 10 minutes.
Place in a blender and puree for 2 minutes
until silky smooth. Strain through a fine-
mesh strainer and chill. Sauce can be
refrigerated for up to 2 days.

*

crab cream

Yields 1/2 cup

1/2 cup small-diced Spanish onion

1 clove garlic, minced

1 tablespoon unsalted butter

3/4 cup shellfish stock (see Basics, p. 269)

3/4 cup heavy cream

• In a saucepan over low heat, sweat onions and garlic in butter until onions are translucent. Add shellfish stock, and cook over high heat until reduced to 1/4 cup. Whisk in cream. Reduce to 1/2 cup. Pass mixture through a chinois. Cool. Crab cream can be refrigerated for up to 2 days.

putting it all together

• Place chipirones on a paper towel to soak up some of the moisture. In a sauté pan over high heat, heat vegetable oil. Once hot remove the pan from the heat and add chipirones. Allow to sizzle for a moment then slowly place the pan back onto the burner. (This process will prevent the pan from catching fire from the water that leaches out of the chipirones.) Sauté chipirones over high heat until slightly seared, about 30 seconds a side. Remove from heat. Add clam juice and squid ink sauce. Place back on the burner and reduce to medium heat. Allow to simmer for 30 seconds and then add butter.

• At the same time, in a separate saucepan over medium heat, combine cooked rice, crab cream, and crabmeat. Cook for about 1 minute until the mixture comes together.

• Arrange chipirones and squid ink sauce in a straight line on each of 4 plates. Place a mold at the end of each line of chipirones and pack with the rice mixture. Remove molds and top with scallions. Drizzle plates with parsley oil.

This recipe has all the same elements you would find in a fish taco eaten on the beach in Baja, California: fried fish, pickled cabbage, and a mayonnaise-based sauce. I added a plantain crust for crunch and a kick of chipotle chile.

The traditional squeeze of lime is still a must.

(NOTE: You'll need to start the pickled cabbage at least a day in advance.)

serves 6

halibut fish tacos with chipotle remoulade and pickled cabbage

1/4 cup vegetable oil, for frying

* 6 servings plantain-crusted halibut

Kosher salt, to taste

Black pepper, to taste

Vegetable oil spray

6 (6-inch) flour tortillas

* 6 tablespoons chipotle remoulade

* 3/4 cup pickled cabbage

6 slices avocado

1 lime, cut into wedges

1 cornhusk, soaked and torn into strips

✳

plantain-crusted halibut

Yields 6 servings

4 cups vegetable oil, For Frying

10 green plantains, peeled and thinly sliced
  (6 ounces Goya brand plantain chips also
  work well)

Kosher salt, to taste

Black pepper, to taste

12 ounces halibut, cut into six 2-ounce
  rectangles

2 cups all-purpose Flour

10 large eggs

• In a Fryer or a deep, heavy-bottomed pan,
heat oil to 375°F. Working in batches, deep-
Fry plantain slices until golden brown.
Remove plantain slices From oil; season with
salt and pepper. Drain and allow to cool. In
a Food processor, process plantain slices
until coarse. Store in a cool dry place. (If
using Goya brand plantain chips, simply
process in Food processor until coarse.)

• Season halibut with salt and pepper. To
bread halibut, arrange 3 large bowls in a
line. Place Flour in First bowl. Whisk eggs in
second bowl. Place plantain crumbs in third
bowl. Coat halibut with Flour and shake oFF
excess. Then coat halibut in egg, shaking
oFF excess. Finally, coat halibut with
plantain crumbs. Shake oFF excess and
place on a tray lined with parchment
paper.

✳

chipotle remoulade

Yields 1/2 cup

1 canned chipotle chile with sauce

1 1/2 teaspoons lime juice

1/4 cup mayonnaise

1 tablespoon capers

3/4 scallion, Finely chopped

2 teaspoons Finely chopped chives

1/2 teaspoon Finely chopped Flat-leaf
  parsley

1/4 teaspoon kosher salt

1/8 teaspoon black pepper

• In a blender, combine chipotle chile puree
and lime juice. Puree until smooth. In a bowl,
combine chipotle mixture with mayonnaise,
capers, scallions, chives, and parsley.
Season with salt and pepper. Remoulade
can be refrigerated For up to 2 days.

*

pickled cabbage

Yields 3/4 cup

2 tablespoons kosher salt

2 tablespoons granulated sugar

1 cup white vinegar

3/4 cup finely shredded red cabbage

• In a plastic container, combine salt, sugar, and vinegar. Add cabbage. Pickle for at least 1 day, covered and refrigerated.

putting it all together

• In a fryer or deep, heavy-bottomed pan, heat oil to 375°F. Fry plantain-crusted halibut until golden brown, about 1 minute. Season with salt and pepper.

• At the same time, heat a cast-iron pan or a griddle plate over medium heat. Spray with vegetable oil to coat. Place tortillas on the pan and heat each side for 15 seconds. Remove the tortillas, but keep the pan over heat.

• Coat 1 side of each tortilla with 1 tablespoon chipotle remoulade. On top of the remoulade place 2 tablespoons pickled cabbage. Add a piece of halibut and an avocado slice to each tortilla. Top halibut with a squeeze of fresh lime, then roll up the tortilla and secure in the middle with a piece of cornhusk. Place the tacos back on the pan or griddle plate and toast each side until slightly browned, about 10 seconds per side.

• Place on a serving plate garnished with remaining lime wedges.

serves 4

dungeness crab guacamole with belgian endive and garlic chips

3 cloves roasted garlic

2 Hass avocados

1/2 pound Dungeness crabmeat, picked

1/4 cup brunoised red onion

1 roasted jalapeño chile, diced small (see Basics, p. 273)

1 plum tomato, seeded and brunoised

2 tablespoons cilantro chiffonade

2 tablespoons lime juice

1/2 teaspoon kosher salt, plus more to taste

2 heads Belgian endive, leaves removed

1/4 cup garlic chips (see Basics, p. 272)

1/4 cup micro cilantro

1 teaspoon extra-virgin olive oil

2 tablespoons lemon oil (see Basics, p. 267)

There's little agreement on what makes a Mexican guacamole recipe authentic. Start with avocado, tomatoes, onion, chiles, cilantro, and lime (though most recipes call for raw garlic, I find the flavor overwhelming), and then experiment with other flavors. Crab is an excellent addition, as are other cooked shellfish and tropical fruits. Almost anything sweet or spicy will work.

putting it all together

• In a molcajete or bowl, mash roasted garlic. Add avocado and mash into roasted garlic. Mix in crabmeat, red onions, jalapeño chiles, tomato, cilantro, and lime juice, and season with 1/2 teaspoon salt.

• Trim off edges of endive leaves and place 3 leaves on each of 4 plates. Form guacamole into quenelles. Place each quenelle on top of an endive leaf. Stick 3 garlic chips into each quenelle.

• Toss cilantro with olive oil and salt, and place on top of guacamole. Drizzle with lemon oil.

Every culture has its own version of the meatball. One of my favorites is the Spanish albondiga, a light, airy meatball made with ground lamb. Considered a homey dish, they are typically served in a tomato sauce. Here I've dressed them up, spiking the rich sauce with foie gras and Spanish sherry.

serves 4

truffled lamb albondigas with sherry-foie gras cream

4 cups vegetable oil, for frying

* 1 1/2 pounds albondiga mixture

Kosher salt, to taste

1/2 cup English peas

* 2 1/2 cups sherry-foie gras cream

1/4 cup chopped black truffle peels (see Sources and Substitutions)

1/4 cup extra-virgin olive oil

1 1/2 ounces manchego cheese, finely grated

1/4 cup micro arugula

*

albondiga mixture

Yields 1 1/2 pounds

2/3 cup small-diced white bread

1/2 cup whole milk

3/4 pound ground lamb

1/4 cup panko bread crumbs

1/3 cup chopped caramelized onion (see
  Basics, p. 271)

2 tablespoons flat-leaf parsley chiffonade

1 tablespoon mint chiffonade

1 teaspoon smoked paprika (see Sources
  and Substitutions)

1 large egg

1/2 teaspoon black pepper

2 teaspoons kosher salt

• Soak bread in milk until milk is absorbed.
In a bowl, fold all ingredients together.

*

sherry–foie gras cream

Yields 2 1/2 cups

3 shallots, sliced

3 cloves garlic, chopped

2 tablespoons vegetable oil

1 cup dry sherry

4 cups heavy cream

1/4 cup onion confit (see Basics, p. 272)

1/4 pound foie gras, chopped

1 1/2 teaspoons kosher salt

• In a saucepan over low heat, sweat
shallots and garlic in oil. Deglaze pan with
sherry. Over medium heat, reduce sherry
mixture to a syrup. Add cream and reduce
mixture by half. Fold pureed onion confit
and foie gras into sherry-cream mixture;
puree everything with a hand blender until
foie gras has melted. Season with salt. Pass
through a chinois. Sherry–foie gras cream
can be refrigerated for up to 2 days.

putting it all together

• Preheat oven to 400°F. In a fryer or large,
heavy-bottomed 4-quart pan, heat oil to
375°F. Using 1-tablespoon portions, roll
albondiga mixture into balls. Working in
batches, fry albondigas for 1 minute, until
browned. Remove albondigas from fryer
and place on a sheet tray; bake 5 minutes.

• Bring a pot of water to a boil, season
heavily with salt. Add peas, boil for 1
minute, then shock in ice water.

• In a saucepan over medium heat combine
albondigas, English peas, and sherry–foie
gras cream. Bring cream to a boil then
reduce to a simmer and cook for about 1
minute, until cream thickens slightly.

• Toss truffle peels in extra-virgin olive oil.

• Spoon albondigas into 4 bowls. Divide
cream among bowls and garnish each with
truffles, manchego, and micro arugula.

Though the taco has Mexican roots, it is very much a part of American food culture, too. You can put almost anything inside a corn tortilla and call it a taco. I've chosen two American favorites: lobster and crab. Be careful not to overstuff the tortillas—you'll want room for garnishes such as sweet potato puree and, for a little Mexican flavor, a spicy mango salsa.

serves 2

maine lobster-and-dungeness crab tacos with sweet potato puree and mango-habanero salsa

6 (4-inch) corn tortillas (see Basics, p. 278)

* 3/4 cup sweet potato puree

* 9 ounces lobster and crab mixture

* 1/2 cup mango-habanero salsa

1/4 cup chive batons

*

sweet potato puree

Yields 1 cup

1 small sweet potato, peeled and chopped

Kosher salt, to taste

2 tablespoons heavy cream

2 tablespoons unsalted butter

1/2 teaspoon ground cinnamon

1 teaspoon granulated sugar

1 teaspoon honey

• Place sweet potatoes in a medium saucepan; cover with water, add salt, and bring to a boil over high heat. Cook until tender. Drain and mash sweet potatoes. In a bowl, while potatoes are still hot, fold in cream and butter. Season with cinnamon, sugar, honey, and salt.

*

lobster and crab mixture

Yields 9 ounces

2 tablespoons unsalted butter

6 ounces poached Maine lobster meat, sliced (see Basics, p. 277)

3 ounces jumbo lump Dungeness crabmeat

Kosher salt, to taste

Black pepper, to taste

• In a sauté pan over medium heat, melt butter. Add lobster and crabmeat and season with salt and pepper. Cook until warm.

*

mango-habanero salsa

Yields 1 cup

1/2 mango, brunoised

1/4 habanero chile, seeded and minced

3 tablespoons finely diced red onion

1 tablespoon finely chopped pickled jalapeño chile rings (see Basics, p. 273)

1 tablespoon finely chopped chives

1 tablespoon finely chopped cilantro

1 tablespoon honey

2 tablespoons lime juice

1 1/2 tablespoons extra-virgin olive oil

1/4 teaspoon kosher salt

1/2 teaspoon granulated sugar

• In a bowl, combine all ingredients. Mix well, adjusting seasoning until salsa is sweet. Salsa can be refrigerated for up to 2 days.

putting it all together

• In a cast-iron skillet over low heat, warm tortillas. In a separate saucepan over medium heat, warm sweet potato puree. Divide tortillas between 2 plates. Top each tortilla with sweet potato puree, lobster and crab mixture, and mango-habanero salsa. Garnish with chives.

Coca is a pizza-like flatbread common in the Catalonia region of Spain. You'll often find it topped with rustic vegetables such as onions and red peppers, though here I've updated the dish with contemporary flavors. When making the crust, I roll it thinner than most Spanish recipes suggest, so that the toppings are the focus of the dish. (NOTE: You'll need to start marinating the duck at least a day in advance.)

serves 4

cocas with marinated duck, cabrales béchamel, and cherry-fig marmalade

* 4 cocas
* 1/2 cup Cabrales béchamel

   7 ounces manchego cheese, shredded

   1/2 cup foie gras mousse (see Sources and Substitutions)

   3 tablespoons heavy cream

   16 leaves baby spinach

* 1 marinated duck breast
* 1/2 cup cherry-fig marmalade

   1 navel orange, zested

*

cocas

Yields 4 cocas

1/2 teaspoon yeast

1/3 cup warm water

1/2 teaspoon honey

1/2 cup pizza flour

1/2 cup all-purpose flour

1 teaspoon kosher salt, plus more for
    sprinkling

1/2 teaspoon granulated sugar

1 teaspoon extra-virgin olive oil, plus more
    for coating

• Bloom yeast in warm water mixed with
honey. In a separate bowl, combine dry
ingredients. Fold yeast mixture into dry
ingredients. Then fold oil into dough. Cover
with plastic wrap and allow to rest in a
warm place until dough doubles in size,
about 2 hours.

• Preheat oven to 300°F. Roll the dough into
four balls. With a rolling pin, flatten each
ball into an oval about 1/4-inch thick and 6
inches long. Using a fork, poke holes into
the dough to prevent air bubbles. Using a
paintbrush, brush the ovals with oil. Season
with salt. Arrange ovals on a sheet pan,
and bake 3 minutes.

*

cabrales béchamel

Yields 1/2 cup

1 tablespoon heavy cream

1/4 pound Cabrales cheese

1/4 cup béchamel (see Basics, p. 274)

• In a saucepan over medium heat, reduce
cream by half then fold in Cabrales. Fold in
béchamel and cool. Cabrales béchamel can
be refrigerated for up to 2 days.

*

marinated duck breast

Yields 1 duck breast

1 teaspoon ground allspice

1/4 stick canela (see Sources and
    Substitutions)

1/2 teaspoon juniper berries (see Sources
    and Substitutions)

1 teaspoon ground star anise

1 navel orange, segmented

1/2 cup grenadine

2 tablespoons molasses

1/2 cup Triple Sec liqueur

1/4 cup soy sauce

1/2 cup brown sugar

1 tablespoon pink curing salt (see Sources
    and Substitutions)

1 Peking duck breast

• In a sauté pan over medium heat, toss
spices to toast. In a bowl, combine all
ingredients except duck. Score duck skin,
then marinate duck breast for 24 hours.

• Remove duck from marinade. In a cast-
iron pan over medium heat, render the
duck skin and cook to medium, about 10
minutes. Remove duck from the pan and
set aside to cool.

putting it all together

• Preheat oven to 500°F; place a pizza stone or sheet tray in the oven to heat. Top each coca with Cabrales béchamel and cover with shredded manchego cheese. Place cocas on the stone and cook until the edges brown and the bottom becomes crisp, 4 to 5 minutes. Remove cocas carefully and cut off any cheese that melted off.

• Mix the foie gras mousse with heavy cream to make it more workable and then spoon into a pastry bag.

• Cut each coca into 4 pieces and place a spinach leaf on each piece. Cut the duck into 1/4-inch-thick slices, and place a slice on each spinach leaf. Garnish each piece of duck with cherry-fig marmalade, foie gras mousse, and orange zest.

＊

cherry-fig marmalade

Yields 1/2 cup

2 tablespoons dried cherries

2 tablespoons dried figs, coarsely chopped

2 tablespoons honey

2 tablespoons agave nectar (see Sources and Substitutions)

2 tablespoons white wine vinegar

2 tablespoons pomegranate juice

• In a saucepan over medium heat, combine all ingredients. Simmer until reduced to 1/2 cup. Remove from heat and puree in a food processor. Mixture will be loose; it will thicken as it cools. Marmalade can be refrigerated for up to 1 week.

These Peruvian rice cakes, spicy with ají amarillo chile paste, are a weakness of mine. They are great on their own, but are even better with other traditional Peruvian flavors such as huacatay, an aromatic herb known as "black mint."

serves 4

tacu-tacu with sous vide lamb loin and huacatay puree

* 4 servings tacu-tacu

  2 tablespoons extra-virgin olive oil

  1 tablespoon vegetable oil

* 1 pound sous vide lamb loin

* 1/2 cup huacatay puree

  1/2 cup toasted black sesame seeds

  1/2 cup huacatay leaves (see Sources and Substitutions)

*

tacu-tacu

Yields 4 servings

3 ounces smoked bacon, cut into lardons

2 cloves garlic, minced

3/4 cup brunoised Spanish onion

1 tablespoon ají amarillo chile paste (see Basics, p. 271)

1/2 pound dried white beans, cooked according to package instructions and pureed

1 cup cooked white rice

2 teaspoons thyme leaves

3 teaspoons oregano leaves

4 tablespoons extra-virgin olive oil

• In a saucepan over low heat, cook bacon until rendered. Add garlic and onion and sweat over low heat until onion is translucent. Add ají amarillo paste and continue cooking over low heat for 5 minutes. Fold in white beans, rice, herbs, and olive oil and cook over low heat for 15 more minutes. Pour onto a sheet tray to cool. Once cool, fill each of 4 small rectangle molds (about 5 inches long by 2 inches wide and 1 inch deep). Cover with plastic wrap and refrigerate. Tacu-tacu can be refrigerated for up to 2 days.

*

sous vide lamb loin

Yields 1 pound

1 pound boneless lamb loin

10 cloves garlic

18 sprigs thyme

8 sprigs rosemary

2 cups extra-virgin olive oil

1 teaspoon kosher salt

• Place lamb loin into a sealable plastic bag with other ingredients. Close bag and squeeze out as much air as possible. (A vacuum sealer works best.) Use a circulator set to 149°F, or fill a pan with 3 gallons water, and over medium heat bring water to 149°F. Keep a thermometer in the water and maintain a constant temperature. Place the bag containing the lamb loin in the water and cook for 18 minutes. (For further explanation of this technique, see Basics, p. 278.) Remove lamb loin from bag.

*

huacatay puree

Yields 1/2 cup

1/4 jalapeño chile, seeded and minced

1/8 habanero chile, seeded and minced

3 tablespoons diced red onion

1/4 clove garlic, minced

1/2 teaspoon vegetable oil

1 tablespoon lemon juice

2 tablespoons heavy cream

1 1/2 tablespoons huacatay paste (see
   Sources and Substitutions)

1 ounce cream cheese

1/4 ounce fresh goat cheese

1 1/2 tablespoons extra-virgin olive oil

• In a saucepan over low heat, sweat jalapeño, habanero, red onion, and garlic in vegetable oil until onion is translucent. Add lemon juice and reduce over medium heat by half. Add cream and huacatay paste and simmer over medium heat for 12 minutes. Then add cream cheese and goat cheese and whisk until melted in. Transfer mixture to a blender and puree. With blender running, add extra-virgin olive oil to emulsify. Puree can be refrigerated for up to 2 days.

putting it all together

• Preheat oven to 350°F. Remove tacu-tacu from molds. Heat olive oil in a cast-iron skillet over high heat and sear tacu-tacu on all sides. Transfer to oven to heat, about 3 minutes.

• At the same time, heat vegetable oil in a cast-iron skillet over high heat, and sear lamb loin on all sides until browned.

• Place one tacu-tacu on each of 4 plates. Slice lamb loin and layer on top of tacu-tacu. Smear a line of huacatay puree next to each tacu-tacu and sprinkle sesame seeds over puree. Garnish the plates with huacatay leaves.

On my most recent trip to San Sebastian, I was inspired by the simple montadito. It's nothing more than an open-faced sandwich, but it can be a great vehicle for Spanish flavors. In this recipe, the topping isn't the traditional cured meat, but a slow-cooked cut of pork garnished with Spanish accents. (NOTE: You'll need to start brining the pork at least three days in advance.)

serves 4

pork belly montaditos with garbanzo bean puree and sherry-honey lacquer

* 4 servings sous vide or braised pork belly

2 tablespoons extra-virgin olive oil

* 4 teaspoons sherry-honey lacquer

8 bias-cut French baguette slices

1 cup garlic oil (see Basics, p. 267)

1 green apple, shaved

1 shallot, shaved

1 tablespoon parsley oil (see Basics, p. 267)

1/2 tablespoon lemon juice

Kosher salt, to taste

* 1/2 cup garbanzo bean puree

*

sous vide or braised pork belly

Yields 4 servings

to brine pork belly:

2 cups apple cider vinegar

1/2 cup honey

1/2 cup molasses

1/2 cup soy sauce

8 cups water

2 cups light brown sugar

2 sticks canela (see Sources and
  Substitutions)

2 star anise

1/4 cup pickling spice

1 teaspoon red pepper flakes

1/4 cup kosher salt

5 cloves garlic

1 1/4 pounds pork belly, skin removed

For braising method only:

1/2 cup vegetable oil

8 cups chopped Spanish onion

1 carrot, chopped

8 cloves garlic

4 cups sherry

16 cups chicken stock (See Basics, see p. 268)

• To brine pork belly: In a plastic container, combine vinegar, honey, molasses, soy sauce, water, brown sugar, spices, and garlic. Mix well until salt and sugar have dissolved. Combine pork belly and brine and refrigerate for 2 days.

• For sous vide method: Remove pork belly from brine. Cut pork belly into 2 even pieces and place into a sealable bag along with 2 cups brining liquid. Close bag and squeeze out as much air as possible. (A vacuum sealer works best.) Use a circulator set to 145°F, or fill a large pan with water, and over low heat, bring water to 145°F. Keep a thermometer in the water and maintain a constant temperature. (For further explanation of this technique, see Basics, p. 278.) Place bag containing pork in the water and cover to reduce evaporation. Cook for 24 hours.

• Alternatively, to make braised pork belly: Preheat oven to 250°F. Remove pork belly from brine and cut into 2 even pieces. In a braising pan over high heat, sear pork on all sides in vegetable oil. Remove pork. In the same pan, combine onions, carrots, and garlic. Caramelize vegetables over high heat. Deglaze saucepan with sherry, scraping the bottom of the pan, and reduce mixture to a syrup. Place pork back into saucepan and add stock to cover. Bring stock to a boil. Remove from heat, cover, and bake 6 1/2 hours.

*

sherry-honey lacquer

Yields 1/2 cup

2 cups sherry vinegar

1 clove garlic

2 teaspoons thyme leaves

1/2 cup acacia honey (see Sources and
    Substitutions)

• In a saucepan over high heat, combine
vinegar, garlic, and thyme. Reduce to 1/2
cup. Add honey and reduce by half. Sherry-
honey lacquer can be refrigerated for up
to 2 days.

*

garbanzo bean puree

Yields 1/2 cup

1/2 cup diced Spanish onion

3 cloves roasted garlic (see Basics, p. 267)

1/2 tablespoon vegetable oil

1/4 cup garbanzo beans, soaked in water
    overnight and drained

1/4 fresh bay leaf

1 cup chicken stock (see Basics, p. 268)

1/4 tablespoon unsalted butter

1/4 teaspoon chopped thyme leaves

1/2 tablespoon lemon juice

2 teaspoons kosher salt

Black pepper, to taste

• In a saucepan over low heat, sweat onions
and garlic in vegetable oil until translucent.
Add beans, bay leaf, and stock and cook
for 1 hour over medium heat. Remove bay
leaf and transfer mixture to a blender.
Add butter, thyme, and lemon juice, and
season with salt and pepper. Puree smooth
and pass through a tamis. Puree can be
refrigerated for up to 2 days.

putting it all together

• Preheat oven to 350°F. Slice pork belly
into 8 portions, 1/4-inch thick. In a cast-iron
skillet over high heat, heat olive oil and
sear 4 portions of pork, about 1 minute per
side. Top each piece of pork with 1
teaspoon sherry-honey lacquer.

• Rub baguette slices with garlic oil and
toast in the oven 5 minutes. In a small bowl,
combine apple and shallot, and toss with
parsley oil and lemon juice. Season with
salt.

• Spread each baguette slice with roasted
garlic–garbanzo bean puree. Place a slice
of pork belly on top of the puree. Top pork
belly with apple-shallot salad.

I was introduced to flautas by Dallas chef Steven Pyles. In the kitchen of Star Canyon, the staff meal was always Tex-Mex and these rolled, fried tacos (you may know them as taquitos) made a frequent appearance. They are typically filled with potato and onion, but your imagination is the limit. I've chosen the familiar combination of duck and orange, but the heat of the chiles is a surprise.

serves 4

duck confit flautas
with poblano-avocado sauce

8 cups vegetable oil, for frying

* 1 1/2 cups duck confit filling

16 (4-inch) corn tortillas (see Basics, p. 278)

* 1 cup poblano-avocado sauce

1/2 cup crema Mexicana (see Basics, p. 274)

1/2 cup shredded romaine lettuce

3 ounces cotilla cheese, grated

4 radishes, julienned

*

duck confit filling

Yields 1 1/2 cups

3/4 cup brunoised Spanish onion

1 clove garlic, minced

2 tablespoons duck fat

1/4 cup guajillo chile paste (see Basics, p. 271)

1 chipotle chile, pureed

2 navel oranges, zested and juiced

1/2 cup chicken stock (see Basics, p. 268)

3 confit duck legs, shredded (see Basics, p. 276)

Kosher salt, to taste

• In a saucepan over low heat, sweat onions and garlic in duck fat until translucent. Add guajillo chile paste, chipotle puree, orange juice, and chicken stock. Cook over high heat until the liquid starts to thicken. Mix in shredded duck. Cook for 5 minutes, then fold in orange zest. Season with salt. Chill.

*

poblano-avocado sauce

Yields 1/2 cup

5 tablespoons large diced Spanish onion

1/4 clove garlic, chopped

1/2 teaspoon vegetable oil

1/4 cup roasted poblano chiles, julienned
   (see Basics, p. 273)

6 tablespoons chicken stock (see Basics,
   p. 268)

2 tablespoons heavy cream

2 tablespoons chopped cilantro

1/2 avocado

1/4 cup whole milk

1/4 teaspoon kosher salt, to taste

• In a saucepan over low heat, sweat onions and garlic in vegetable oil until translucent.

Add poblanos and cover with chicken stock and heavy cream. Over high heat, reduce mixture by half. Remove from heat and cool. In a blender, puree poblano mixture. Add cilantro then avocado, pureeing until smooth. Season with salt. Sauce can be refrigerated for up to 24 hours.

putting it all together

• In a fryer or a deep, heavy-bottomed 4-quart pan, heat oil to 375°F. Make flautas by wrapping 3 tablespoons duck confit filling in 2 slightly overlapping tortillas. Secure with a toothpick. Fry flautas until golden brown, about 1 minute.

• Sauce 4 plates with poblano-avocado sauce. Arrange 2 flautas on each plate. Drizzle each plate with crema Mexicana and garnish with romaine, cotilla cheese, and radishes.

In Spain, white asparagus is a finger food, dipped, like a french fry, into mayonnaise. It's surprisingly decadent, and I wanted to magnify that feeling in this recipe. In place of plain mayonnaise I serve truffle aïoli. The real key, however, is getting the freshest white asparagus available, and cooking it quickly.

serves 4

white asparagus
with truffle aïoli
and aged manchego

2 tablespoons chopped black truffle peels (see Sources and Substitutions)

2 tablespoons extra-virgin olive oil

12 stalks white asparagus

* 1/4 cup truffle aïoli

1 ounce aged manchego cheese, shaved

2 tablespoons flat-leaf parsley chiffonade

*

truffle aïoli

Yields 1 cup

1 large egg yolk

1 teaspoon lemon juice

1/2 clove garlic, zested

1/2 cup vegetable oil, as needed

1/4 cup black truffle oil, as needed (see Sources and Substitutions)

1/2 cup dried black trumpet mushrooms (see Sources and Substitutions)

1 teaspoon finely chopped black truffle peels (see Sources and Substitutions)

1 teaspoon kosher salt

• In a bowl, combine egg yolk, lemon juice, and garlic, and whisk until smooth. While whisking, slowly add vegetable oil until emulsified, then slowly whisk in truffle oil. Aïoli can be stored in refrigerator for up to 1 week.

• Place mushrooms in a cup and run warm water over them until they are rinsed and become soft. Then place the mushrooms on a towel to dry before finely chopping. Fold mushrooms and chopped black truffle peels into aïoli. Season with salt.

putting it all together

• Preheat broiler. Marinate truffle peels in olive oil. Peel asparagus. Bring a pot of water to a boil and blanch asparagus 1 minute. Shock in ice water. Arrange asparagus on a tray and place under the broiler for 1 minute. Bunch asparagus into groups of 3 stalks and cover with truffle aïoli, leaving the tips of the asparagus exposed. Place asparagus under the broiler until aïoli browns, about 20 seconds.

• Smear a plate with remaining truffle aïoli then place asparagus on top. Garnish with manchego, parsley, and marinated truffle peels.

Pasteles are Puerto Rico's answer to the Mexican tamale—but they don't include corn. Instead, grated plantains and yucca are used. In this version of a pastel, I also draw on influences from Cuban classics, shrimp enchilado and a rich black bean broth.

serves 4

puerto rican pasteles with black bean broth and shrimp enchilado sauce

* 2 cups black bean broth

* 4 pasteles

* 1 cup shrimp enchilado sauce

  5 radishes, finely julienned

  8 cherry tomatoes, quartered

  2 tablespoons lemon juice

  1/4 cup extra-virgin olive oil

  Kosher salt, to taste

  Black pepper, to taste

  4 cups vegetable oil, for frying

  4 culantro leaves (see Sources and Substitutions)

*

pasteles

Yields 4 pasteles

2 1/4 cups diced Spanish onion

1 green bell pepper, diced

5 cloves garlic, chopped

2 teaspoons vegetable oil

2 teaspoons ground cumin

1 green plantain, finely grated

1 yucca, peeled and finely grated

1/2 cup cilantro, finely chopped

1 teaspoon baking powder

1 teaspoon kosher salt

4 banana leaves, cut into 6-inch squares
 (see Sources and Substitutions)

• In a saucepan over high heat sauté onion,
bell pepper, and garlic in vegetable oil for
10 minutes. Transfer vegetables to a
blender and puree until smooth.

• In a sauté pan over medium heat, toast
cumin, tossing the pan constantly.

• In a bowl, combine vegetable puree, cumin,
and remaining ingredients except banana
leaves. Fold ingredients together until
thoroughly mixed.

• Place banana leaves in a steamer for 1
minute to make them more pliable. Remove
leaves and top each leaf with 1/2 cup
vegetable mixture. Fold ends of each leaf
to form 4-inch squares. Wrap squares
individually in plastic wrap and steam for
40 minutes.

*

black bean broth

Yields 2 cups

1/4 pound dried black beans, picked and
 soaked overnight in water

2 cups water

1 bay leaf

1/4 teaspoon white vinegar

1/2 teaspoon kosher salt

3 cloves roasted garlic (see Basics, p. 267)

1/4 cup onion confit (see Basics, p. 272)

1/4 roasted green bell pepper (see Basics,
 p. 273)

4 1/2 tablespoons extra-virgin olive oil

1/2 teaspoon dried oregano

• Rinse beans. In a saucepan over high heat,
combine beans, water, bay leaf, vinegar, and
salt. Bring mixture to a boil. Reduce heat
and simmer until beans are slightly tender,
about 1 hour.

• In a blender, combine garlic, onion confit,
and bell pepper. Puree until smooth. In a
saucepan over high heat, heat olive oil. Add
vegetable puree then turn down heat to
medium. Add beans along with their cooking
liquid and oregano and simmer 30 minutes.
Once the beans are fully cooked, puree
with a hand blender. Broth should remain
slightly chunky. Broth can be refrigerated
for 2 to 3 days.

*

shrimp enchilado sauce

Yields 1 cup

2 teaspoons extra-virgin olive oil

1 1/2 tablespoons brunoised Spanish onion

2 1/2 cachucha chiles, seeded and brunoised
(see Sources and Substitutions)

1/4 jalapeño chile, seeded and brunoised

1/4 red bell pepper, brunoised

1/4 green bell pepper, brunoised

1 clove garlic, minced

2 tablespoons white wine

1/4 tomato, chopped

1/2 teaspoon tomato paste

1 1/2 tablespoons tomato juice

1/4 cup white shrimp stock (see Basics, p. 270)

2 ounces 26/30 shrimp, peeled, deveined,
tails removed, finely chopped

1/2 teaspoon kosher salt

White pepper, to taste

• In a braising pan over high heat, heat
olive oil. Sauté onions, chiles, and bell
peppers until onions are translucent, about
2 minutes. Add garlic and sauté for
another minute. Deglaze with wine. Reduce
heat to low and add tomatoes, tomato
paste, tomato juice, and shrimp stock.
Cook 10 minutes, stirring occasionally. Add
chopped shrimp and season with salt and
white pepper. Cook 2 minutes. Transfer to
a storage container and place in an ice
bath. Sauce can be refrigerated for up to
2 days.

putting it all together

• In a saucepan over medium heat, heat
black bean broth. At the same time, return
pasteles to the steamer until hot, about 5
minutes. In a separate saucepan over
medium heat, heat enchilado sauce.

• In a bowl, toss radishes and cherry
tomatoes with lemon juice, extra-virgin
olive oil, salt, and pepper.

• In a fryer or a deep, heavy-bottomed
4-quart pan, heat vegetable oil to 375°F.
Place culantro leaves into fryer for 5
seconds then remove and drain.

• In the bottom of each of 4 shallow bowls
place 1/2 cup black bean broth. Remove the
pasteles from the plastic and banana leaf,
place in the middle of each bowl, and top
with 1/4 cup enchilado sauce. Use radish-
cherry tomato salad as a garnish around
the pasteles. Top each pastel with a fried
culantro leaf.

the tradition of corn

We are all familiar with tamales, sopes, humitas, arepas,

and, of course, tortillas. Corn is an indispensable

ingredient in South American and Mexican cooking, and

one that sets those cuisines apart from their Spanish roots.

It makes sense: Corn in the Americas is abundant, inexpensive, filling,

and tasty. (And where corn is less prevalent, as in Puerto Rico,

grated plantains and yucca are the basis of many similar recipes.)

The Latin culinary tradition is full of ways to make the most of

these starchy vegetables. My challenge is not to reinvent these

time-tested recipes, but to find new ways to use these common

preparations.   •   I think of corn as a vehicle for other flavors, and

those flavors don't have to be traditional. Tamales are delicious

stuffed with classic roasted pork, but sopes are as appetizing

topped with a light almost-American crab salad. When creating any

recipe, I look for balance. In these recipes, the corn grounds the

dish, providing a neutral background for surprising flavors.

Cornhusk-wrapped tamales are a staple of the Mexican diet. The secret to the perfect melt-in-your-mouth corn tamale is lard—the more, the better. These soft corn pillows are then stuffed with flavorful fillings and steamed. Here I use a classic Yucatán recipe: pork slow-roasted (for 8 hours) with oranges and complex spices.

serves 4

ancho tamales with yucatán pork, charred tomatillo sauce, and criolla cebolla

* ★ 4 ancho tamales
* ★ 3/4 cup pork sauce
* ★ 1 cup charred tomatillo sauce
* ★ 4 servings cochinita pork
* ★ 6 tablespoons criolla cebolla

*

ancho tamales

Yields 4 tamales

6 tablespoons lard

1/2 red bell pepper, brunoised

3 tablespoons brunoised Spanish onion

1/4 clove garlic, minced

5 tablespoons ancho chile paste (see
   Basics, p. 271)

1/4 pound masa harina (see Sources and
   Substitutions)

1/2 cup chicken stock (see Basics, p. 268)

1/4 teaspoon baking powder

1 1/2 tablespoons kosher salt

4 cornhusks, soaked in water

• In a saucepan over high heat, melt lard.
Sauté bell pepper, onion, garlic, and ancho
chile paste in lard. Once vegetables have
softened, puree them in a blender until
smooth to form a sofrito.

• In a mixer, combine masa harina and
chicken stock. Fold in sofrito, baking
powder, and salt. Divide masa into 4
portions. Wrap 1 soaked cornhusk around
each masa portion, tying off each end with
a strip of cornhusk. Place in the
refrigerator until ready to use. Tamales
can be refrigerated for up to 2 days.

*

pork sauce

Yields 3/4 cup

1 plum tomato

1 cup chopped Spanish onion

1/2 clove roasted garlic (see Basics, p. 267)

1 tablespoon vegetable oil

2 tablespoons cochinita marinade

3/4 cup pork cooking liquid, from cochinita
   pork recipe

1/4 cup orange juice

1/2 teaspoon kosher salt

• Char plum tomato over an open flame
until blistered. In a saucepan over high
heat, sauté onions and garlic in vegetable
oil until slightly colored. Add cochinita
marinade and half of the pork cooking
liquid. Cook mixture for 3 minutes, then
add orange juice and charred tomato.
Reduce heat to a simmer and add
remaining pork cooking liquid. Reduce
mixture by half. Puree in a blender until
smooth, and season with salt.

*

charred tomatillo sauce

Yields 1 cup

1/4 large Spanish onion

1 clove garlic

1/4 jalapeño chile

3 tomatillos

1/8 teaspoon ground cumin

2 tablespoons vegetable oil

1/2 bay leaf

1/8 teaspoon dried thyme

2 black peppercorns

1 teaspoon dried oregano

1/4 cup vegetable stock (see Basics, p. 270)

3 tablespoons chopped cilantro

1 tablespoon extra-virgin olive oil

1 1/2 teaspoons kosher salt

• Char vegetables on a grill or under a broiler until browned, then roughly chop. In a sauté pan over high heat, toss cumin for 1 minute to toast. In a separate saucepan over high heat, heat vegetable oil. Sauté vegetables with cumin, bay leaf, thyme, black peppercorns, and oregano, 10 minutes. Then add stock. Bring mixture to a boil over high heat. Then reduce to a simmer for 20 minutes. Allow to cool. Puree sauce in a blender with the cilantro until smooth. While pureeing, slowly add olive oil to emulsify. Season with salt.

*

cochinita pork

Yields 4 servings

1 pound pork butt

5 cloves garlic, sliced

1/4 cup kosher salt

1/2 cup cochinita marinade (see following recipe)

5 avocado leaves (see Sources and Substitutions)

5 bay leaves

5 sprigs oregano

2 large banana leaves (see Sources and Substitutions)

4 cups chicken stock (see Basics, p. 268)

• Preheat oven to 225°F. Puncture pork butt with a boning knife and insert garlic into punctures. Season pork butt well with salt, and coat with cochinita marinade. Cover pork butt with avocado leaves, bay leaves, oregano, and finally, wrap it entirely in banana leaves.

• To a deep pan with a wire rack, add chicken stock. Place pork butt in pan and cover with foil. Place in oven to roast 8 hours. Let rest before shredding meat; reserve cooking liquid from interior pan for pork sauce. Pork can be refrigerated for up to 2 days.

cochinita marinade

Yields 3/4 cup

1/8 brick achiote (see Sources and Substitutions)

1/4 large Spanish onion

2 cloves garlic

1 chipotle chile

1 tablespoon white vinegar

1 1/2 teaspoons ground allspice

1 tablespoon Mexican oregano (see Sources and Substitutions)

3 tablespoons orange juice

1 tablespoon lime juice

• Combine all ingredients in a blender and puree smooth. Marinade can be refrigerated for up to 2 days.

✳

criolla cebolla

Yields 1 cup

1 2/3 finely julienned red onion

2/3 jalapeño chile, finely julienned

2 tablespoons finely julienned cilantro

1/4 cup lime juice

1/4 cup extra-virgin olive oil

1 teaspoon granulated sugar

1/2 teaspoon kosher salt, to taste

• Wash onions in cold water. In a bowl, combine onions with jalapeño chiles, cilantro, lime juice, and olive oil. Season with sugar and salt. Criolla cebolla can be refrigerated for up to 1 week.

putting it all together

• While tamales are cooking, pour pork sauce and charred tomatillo sauce into separate small saucepans and bring both mixtures to a boil. Once the pork sauce boils, add shredded cochinita pork, reduce heat to low, and simmer 1 minute. Once the charred tomatillo sauce boils, reduce to low heat.

• Sauce 4 plates with charred tomatillo sauce. Remove tamales from the steamer, and cut a slice in the top of each one. Open the tamales up slightly and fill with pork sauce. Top each tamale with criolla cebolla.

I grew up eating Ecuadorian arepas, but the white-corn cakes will also taste familiar to anyone who has spent time below the Mason-Dixon Line: White cornmeal is also the basis for grits. Although this recipe draws from Ecuador, Venezuela, and Cuba, it tastes like something you might find at a Southern barbecue.

serves 4

arepas with oxtail ropa vieja and avocado espuma

1/4 cup vegetable oil, for frying

* 4 arepas

Kosher salt, to taste

2 ounces uncooked smoked bacon

* 3/4 pound oxtail ropa vieja with 1/4 cup jus

4 thin slices green heirloom tomato

4 thin slices red heirloom tomato

* 1/2 cup avocado espuma

1/2 cup micro arugula

2 tablespoons extra-virgin olive oil

*

arepas

Yields 4 arepas

1 cup instant arepas flour (see Sources and
  Substitutions)

1/2 teaspoon kosher salt

1 1/4 cups hot water

1/4 cup unsalted butter, melted

1/4 cup queso fresco

• In a bowl, combine flour and salt. Add
water and butter to flour mixture while
stirring. Mix thoroughly. Add queso fresco
and mix to combine. Take the dough out of
the bowl and knead until pliable. Using a 3-
inch ring mold, form four 1/2-inch-thick
disks.

*

oxtail ropa vieja

Yields 1 1/4 pounds

3 pounds oxtail

1/4 cup vegetable oil

1 large Spanish onion, 1/2 chopped, 1/2
  julienned

1/2 large carrot, chopped

9 cloves garlic, 6 whole, 3 julienned

1 1/2 teaspoon kosher salt

1/4 cup plus 1/3 cup tomato paste

3 cups red wine

4 cups veal stock (see Basics, p. 270)

3 guindilla chiles (see Sources and Substitutions)
  or 1 teaspoon red pepper flakes

1 tablespoon black peppercorns

10 sprigs thyme

1 yellow bell pepper, julienned

• Preheat oven to 325°F. In a braising pan
over medium-high heat, sear oxtails on all
sides in 2 tablespoons vegetable oil. Remove
oxtails and place in a deep pot. Add
chopped onion, carrots, and whole garlic
cloves to the braising pan and season with
salt. Over high heat sauté the vegetables
until browned. Add 1/4 cup tomato paste
and cook for an additional 5 minutes. Add
red wine and veal stock to deglaze,
scraping bottom of pan to loosen
caramelized bits. Bring mixture to a boil.
Remove from heat and pour mixture over
oxtails. Add guindilla chiles (or red pepper
flakes), peppercorns, and thyme. Cover
tightly with foil and cook for 3 hours.
Remove oxtails from the liquid and shred
the meat. Strain jus and reserve.

• In a large braising pan over low heat,
sweat julienned onions and yellow bell
peppers in vegetable oil until soft. Add
julienned garlic and 1/3 cup tomato paste,
and continue to sweat for an additional 5
minutes. Add reserved oxtail jus and bring
to a boil; reduce heat to a simmer. Reduce
mixture until the sauce has thickened to
nappé (thick enough to coat the back of a
spoon). Add shredded oxtail and cook for
an additional 10 minutes over low heat.
Pour mixture out onto a sheet tray and
refrigerate to cool. Ropa vieja can be
frozen for up to 1 week.

*

avocado espuma

Yields 1 cup

1/2 avocado, peeled and chopped

1/2 jalapeño chile, seeded and diced

1 tablespoon cilantro leaves

1 1/2 teaspoons lemon juice

1 tablespoon heavy cream

1/4 cup whole milk

1/2 teaspoon granulated sugar

1 1/2 teaspoons kosher salt

• In a blender, combine avocado, jalapeño, cilantro, and lemon juice, and puree. With blender running, add cream and milk and process until smooth. Season with sugar and salt. Use immediately.

putting it all together

• Preheat oven to 350°F. To a sauté pan add vegetable oil to just cover the bottom of the pan. Heat oil over medium heat until it starts to sizzle. Add the arepas and fry until golden brown, about 1 minute on each side. Remove arepas, drain, and season with salt. Split each arepa by cutting in half horizontally.

• Cut each slice of bacon on the bias into 2 triangles. Arrange on a baking sheet and cook in oven until crisp.

• In a saucepan over medium heat, heat oxtail ropa vieja with jus.

• Place 2 arepa halves on each of 4 plates. On each plate, top one arepa half with oxtail mixture. Place a slice of green tomato and a slice of red tomato over the oxtail. Top with a bacon triangle, avocado espuma, and micro arugula tossed in olive oil.

Humitas are the Ecuadorian version of Mexican tamales. They always remind me of my mother and grandmother, who often made them. You can find different recipes throughout South America, but the classic is stuffed with mild white queso fresco. I've used the cheese as a sauce, and I've added more corn with a garnish of popcorn shoots.

serves 4

sweet corn humitas with truffle aïoli and queso de cabra emulsion

* 4 humitas
* 1 cup truffle aïoli
  1 cup popcorn shoots (see Sources and Substitutions)
* 4 teaspoons queso de cabra emulsion
  8 thin slices black truffle (see Sources and Substitutions)

*

humitas

Yields 4

2 cups sweet corn kernels, pureed

3 1/2 ounces queso fresco, grated

1 cup corn stock (see Basics, p. 269)

1 teaspoon baking powder

1 cup white corn flour

1 tablespoon granulated sugar

2 teaspoons kosher salt

4 dried cornhusks, soaked in water

• In a bowl, combine corn puree, cheese, corn stock, baking powder, and corn flour. Season with sugar and salt. Fill each cornhusk with 1/2 cup corn mixture. Wrap the cornhusk around the filling. Place humitas in a steamer to cook, 20 minutes. Remove from steamer and set aside until needed.

*

truffle aïoli

Yields 1 cup

1 large egg yolk

1 teaspoon lemon juice

1/2 clove garlic, zested

1 teaspoon kosher salt

1/2 cup vegetable oil, as needed

1/4 cup black truffle oil, as needed (see Sources and Substitutions)

1/2 cup dried black trumpet mushrooms (see Sources and Substitutions)

1 teaspoon finely chopped black truffle peels (see Sources and Substitutions)

• In a bowl, combine egg yolk, lemon juice, garlic, and salt and whisk until smooth. While whisking, slowly add vegetable oil until emulsified, then slowly whisk in truffle oil. Aïoli can be stored in refrigerator for up to 1 week.

• Place mushrooms in a cup and run warm water over them until they are rinsed and become soft. Then place the mushrooms on a towel to dry before finely chopping. Fold mushrooms and chopped black truffle peels into aïoli. Season with salt.

*

queso de cabra emulsion

Yields about 1 1/2 cups

1 ounce fresh queso de cabra cheese

1/4 cup whole milk

1/4 cup heavy cream

Kosher salt, to taste

1/4 teaspoon soy lecithin (see Sources and Substitutions)

• In a saucepan over medium heat, combine cheese, milk, and cream. Whisk mixture until cheese melts. Pour into a blender and puree until smooth. Pass through a chinois and season with salt. Add soy lecithin and stir until dissolved. Use immediately.

putting it all together

• Preheat broiler. Place 4 humitas back into the steamer to reheat, 2 to 3 minutes. Remove from steamer and open cornhusks. Top each with a 1/4 cup truffle aïoli. Place humitas under a broiler to brown truffle aïoli. Remove and place on a serving plate.

• Place popcorn shoots atop humitas. Using a hand blender, buzz queso de cabra emulsion until frothy. Dot a line of the emulsion next to humitas. Place truffles between dots of emulsion.

Sopes, like tamales and tortillas, are made with Mexico's favorite ingredient: corn. These small corn masa "boats" can be filled with a variety of toppings. Here I've used a fresh crab salad to offset the dense corn.

serves 4

sopes with crab salpicon

4 cups vegetable oil, for frying

★ 8 sopes

Kosher salt, to taste

8 avocado slices

★ 2 cups crab salpicon

3 radishes, julienned

1 tablespoon espelette powder (see Sources and Substitutions)

∗

sopes

Yields 8 sopes

2 cups masa harina (see Sources and
    Substitutions)

1 tablespoon lard

1 teaspoon kosher salt

1 1/2 cups warm water

• In a bowl, combine masa harina, lard, and
salt. Knead well, adding warm water
gradually until dough is soft and smooth.
Form dough into 8 small disks, 2 inches in
diameter and 1/2 inch thick. Form a well in
each disk by pulling the dough up to make a
wall around the edge.

∗

crab salpicon

Yields 2 cups

1/2 pound lump crabmeat

1/4 cup mayonnaise

1/4 cup sour cream

1/2 plum tomato, finely diced

6 tablespoons finely diced red onion

2 tablespoons finely chopped cilantro

1/2 jalapeño chile, seeded and finely diced

2 tablespoons finely chopped chives

1 tablespoon lime juice

Kosher salt, to taste

• In a bowl, combine all ingredients and mix
well.

putting it all together

• In a fryer or a deep, heavy-bottomed
4-quart pan, heat vegetable oil to 375°F.
Working in batches, fry sopes until they
just start to brown, about 1 minute. Drain
sopes and season with salt.

• Lay a slice of avocado in the bottom of
each sope. Shape salpicon into 8 quenelles
and place one on each avocado slice.
Garnish each with radish and espelette.

the tradition of empanadas

The word empanada comes from the Spanish verb "empanar," to bake in pastry, and that basic idea—stuffed dough—is one of the only things empanadas have in common as you travel from Spain through Latin America to Ecuador and Argentina. In my travels I've eaten savory empanadas and sweet ones, baked empanadas and fried. They can be shaped from any dough I can cook up—from puff pastry to plantain—and stuffed with any filling I can imagine, which makes the simple snack a blank slate for your creativity. • The traditional Spanish empanada is a savory pie, filled with cooked onions and peppers, eggplant, or tomatoes, and cut into wedges. But, while the empanada may trace its origins to Spain, the South American–style empanada—smaller, crisp turnovers—is better known. In Argentina, those empanadas are typically baked with a buttery wheat-flour crust and a meat filling. In Ecuador, the crust is more commonly oil-based. There, plantain, rice, or white-corn dough is stuffed with vegetables or meat and quickly fried. • But those are only traditions, not rules. I sometimes fry my Argentinean empanadas to achieve a crisp, flaky crust, and stuff my Ecuadorian empanadas—made with my grandmother's smooth plantain dough—with a Spanish-style vegetable filling.

In Argentina, empanadas are typically baked, not fried. That's why you'll find butter in this saffron dough. The filling in this recipe isn't what you'd find on the streets of Buenos Aires (ground beef or ham and cheese are the most common), but short ribs remind me of the rich beef dishes served throughout the country.

serves 5

saffron empanadas
with braised short ribs
and cabrales crème fraîche

* 1 1/4 cups braised short ribs

1/2 cup short-rib braising liquid, from braised short ribs recipe

* 1 recipe saffron dough

3 ounces Cabrales cheese

1 large egg, beaten

* 6 tablespoons Cabrales crème fraîche

12 confit cherry tomatoes, halved (see Basics, p. 272)

1/4 cup pickled jalapeño chile rings (see Basics, p. 273)

6 tablespoons oregano oil (see Basics, p. 267)

*

braised short ribs

Yields 1 1/2 cups shredded meat and 1/2 cup
  braising liquid

2 pounds beef short ribs

1/4 cup vegetable oil

5 cups large diced Spanish onions

1 carrot, sliced

2 stalks celery, chopped

10 cloves garlic

1 tablespoon black peppercorns

1 cup tomato paste

2 beefsteak tomatoes, chopped

4 cups red wine

6 cups beef stock

6 sprigs thyme

2 sheets gelatin

• In a braising pan over high heat, sear
short ribs in oil on all sides. Remove ribs
and place in a baking pan. In same braising
pan, add onions, carrots, celery, garlic, and
peppercorns. Over high heat, cook
vegetables, stirring frequently, until
caramelized, about 20 minutes. Add tomato
paste and tomatoes, and cook over high
heat until paste is caramelized, about 10
minutes. Add wine and deglaze pan,
scraping the bottom to loosen caramelized
pieces. Add beef stock and bring to a boil.

• Preheat oven to 325°F. Pour beef stock
mixture over the short ribs and add thyme.
Be sure that the short ribs are completely
covered with liquid. Cover tightly and braise
in oven for 3 hours. Take ribs out of the
liquid; strain off liquid, reserving 1/2 cup. Bloom
gelatin in ice water. Squeeze out excess
water and mix gelatin with braising liquid.

• While ribs are still hot, shred the meat
and set aside to cool. Braised short ribs
can be refrigerated for up to 2 days or
frozen for up to 2 weeks.

*

saffron dough

Yields dough for 5 empanadas

1 cup all-purpose flour

1/4 cup unsalted butter, melted

2 tablespoons water

1/2 teaspoon saffron threads

• In a bowl, combine all ingredients and mix
well. Form five 3-tablespoon portions of
dough and set on a tray lined with
parchment paper. Cover with plastic wrap.
Set aside for 20 minutes. Dough can be
stored in refrigerator for up to 3 days.

*

cabrales crème fraîche

Yields 6 tablespoons

1/4 cup Cabrales cheese

3 tablespoons crème fraîche

2 teaspoons kosher salt

• In a bowl, combine all ingredients. Mix well.

putting it all together

• Preheat oven to 350°F. To make empanadas,
combine shredded short ribs and braising
liquid. Using a tortilla press lined with
plastic wrap, or a rolling pin, flatten dough
balls. In the middle of each one, place 1/4
cup short rib filling and 2 tablespoons
Cabrales cheese. Fold the empanada in half,
and press the edges with a fork to seal.
Brush with egg. Bake for 15 minutes.

• Divide Cabrales crème fraîche among 5
plates. Cut empanadas in half and place 2
halves cut side down on each plate so that
they stand up. Garnish with tomato confit,
pickled jalapeño rings, and oregano oil.

My grandmother taught me the secret to these Ecuadorian snacks. The plantain dough isn't hard to make, if you know the proper technique: You have to knead the dough thoroughly. This makes it more malleable and easier to quickly roll out and fill.

serves 4

green plantain empanadas with spinach-manchego filling and artichoke escabeche

* 1/2 cup spinach-manchego filling

* 4 verde dough rounds

  8 cups vegetable oil, for frying

  Kosher salt, to taste

* 1 1/2 cups artichoke escabeche

*

spinach-manchego filling

Yields 1 cup

1/4 pound baby spinach

2 cloves garlic, minced

1 tablespoon vegetable oil

1 teaspoon kosher salt

5 cloves roasted garlic (see Basics, p. 267)

1/2 cup béchamel (see Basics, p. 274)

1 tablespoon whole milk

2 ounces manchego cheese, grated

• In a sauté pan over high heat, sauté spinach and garlic in vegetable oil. Season with salt. Strain off all excess liquid, roughly chop spinach, and place in a bowl. Mash up roasted garlic and add to spinach.

• In a saucepan over medium heat, combine béchamel and milk. Pour béchamel mixture over the spinach. Add manchego. Mix thoroughly and cool. Spinach-manchego filling can be refrigerated for up to 2 days.

*

verde dough

Yields 4 rounds

1 green plantain

Kosher salt, to taste

• Make 2 slits down each side of plantain and soak in warm water, about 20 minutes. Peel plantain. Boil plantain in water until very tender, about 45 minutes. Put boiled plantain through ricer twice, and season with salt. Pack riced plantain into 4 balls. Place the balls in a bowl, cover, and allow to cool for 15 minutes.

• Remove from bowl and knead each ball until pliable. The dough should break down and then come back together 3 times. Using a tortilla press lined with plastic wrap, or a rolling pin, flatten each ball. Cover with plastic wrap so the dough doesn't dry out. Use immediately.

✳

artichoke escabeche

Yields 1 1/2 cups

2 tablespoons piquillo chiles, julienned (see
   Sources and Substitutions)

1/4 cup thinly sliced confit artichoke (see
   Basics, p. 271)

1/4 shallot, thinly sliced

2 teaspoons honey

2 tablespoons sherry vinegar

2 tablespoons extra-virgin olive oil

1 tablespoon finely chopped flat-leaf
   parsley

1/2 teaspoon kosher salt

1/8 teaspoon black pepper

• In a bowl, fold all ingredients together.
Escabeche can be refrigerated for up to 1
week.

putting it all together

• To make empanadas, place 2 tablespoons
spinach-manchego filling in the middle of
each of 4 verde dough rounds. Fold the
dough in half, and press the edges of the
dough with a fork to seal the empanada.

• In a fryer or a deep, heavy-bottomed
4-quart pan, heat vegetable oil to 375°F.
Drop empanadas into oil and fry until
slightly browned, 1 to 1 1/2 minutes. Remove
from oil and drain. Season with salt.

• Divide artichoke escabeche among 4 plates.
Cut each empanada in half and place the 2
halves cut side down on each plate so that
the empanada halves stand up.

pescados

y mariscos

fish & shellfish

The term sous vide can be intimidating, but the low-
temperature cooking process is a surprisingly
simple way to infuse fish with intense flavor—very
similar to poaching. This old-world cooking style is
gaining new popularity among avant-garde chefs,
but I like to use it with familiar Spanish flavors.

serves 4

sous vide halibut
with chorizo croquettes
and saffron emulsion

8 cups vegetable oil, for frying

★ 4 chorizo croquettes

★ 4 servings sous vide halibut

★ 1/2 cup saffron emulsion

4 serrano ham chips (see Basics, p. 277)

*

chorizo croquettes

Yields 8 croquettes

1/2 pound Idaho potatoes, peeled

1/2 tablespoon vegetable oil

3 ounces chorizo de Bilbao, diced small

1/4 cup small-diced Spanish onion

1 clove garlic, minced

1 tablespoon unsalted butter

3/4 cup all-purpose flour

1/2 cup whole milk

3 1/2 sheets gelatin

1/8 teaspoon smoked paprika (see Sources
    and Substitutions)

3 large eggs

1 cup finely ground bread crumbs

• In a saucepan over high heat, cook potatoes in enough water to cover, until tender. Strain out water and pass potatoes through a ricer. Set aside.

• In a saucepan over low heat, heat oil and render chorizo. Add onion and garlic, and continue to cook over low heat until onion is translucent. Add butter and melt. Add 1/4 cup flour and cook 5 minutes. Stir in milk and cook over low heat until thickened, about 20 minutes.

• Bloom gelatin in ice water; squeeze out excess water. Add bloomed gelatin, riced potatoes, and paprika to chorizo mixture. Mix thoroughly. Pour onto a sheet pan and place in the refrigerator to set, about 1 hour. When set, cut into 2-inch-by-3-inch pieces.

• To bread croquettes, arrange 3 large bowls in a line. Place 1/2 cup flour in first bowl. Whisk eggs in second bowl. Place bread crumbs in third bowl. Drop croquettes into flour, shaking bowl until croquettes are completely coated. Remove croquettes from flour, shaking off excess, and put into bowl with eggs. Shake bowl until croquettes are completely covered in egg. Remove croquettes from egg, shake off excess, and put into bowl with bread crumbs. Shake bowl until croquettes are evenly coated. Remove croquettes from bread crumbs, shake off excess and place on tray lined with parchment paper. Refrigerate, uncovered. Breaded croquettes can be refrigerated for up to 3 days or frozen for up to 1 week.

saffron emulsion

Yields about 2 cups

1/2 shallot, chopped

1 clove garlic, chopped

1 teaspoon extra-virgin olive oil

1 teaspoon saffron threads

2 tablespoons white wine

1 cup heavy cream

1/2 teaspoon kosher salt, to taste

1/4 teaspoon soy lecithin (see Sources and
  Substitutions)

• In a saucepan over low heat, sweat shallots and garlic in olive oil until shallots are translucent. Add saffron and cook over low heat until the saffron has bloomed, releasing its color, about 5 minutes. Deglaze pan with white wine, and reduce mixture by half over high heat. Add cream and bring to a boil. Add salt to taste. Remove mixture from heat and stir in soy lecithin. Emulsion can be refrigerated for up to 1 week. Before using, foam emulsion with a hand blender.

*

sous vide halibut

Yields 4 servings

1 pound halibut, skin and pin bones removed

4 cloves garlic

4 sprigs thyme

1 cup extra-virgin olive oil

2 teaspoons kosher salt

• Cut fish into 4 equal pieces and place in a sealable plastic bag with garlic, thyme, olive oil, and salt. Close bag and squeeze out as much air as possible. (A vacuum sealer works best.)

• In a circulator or a saucepan filled with water over medium heat, bring water to 140°F. Keep a thermometer in the water and maintain a constant temperature. (For further explanation of this technique, see Basics, p. 278.) Place the bag containing the halibut in the water and cook 9 minutes.

putting it all together

• In a fryer or a deep, heavy-bottomed 4-quart pan over high heat, heat oil to 375°F. Fry chorizo croquettes in oil until golden brown. Drain croquettes on paper towels.

• Place 1 croquette on each of 4 plates. Remove fish from bag, reserving liquid. Place a piece of fish on top of each croquette, and divide the liquid among the plates. Spoon saffron emulsion over each piece of fish. Slide serrano ham chips into the fish as a garnish.

Mexican mole verde is a classic tomatillo-based sauce. While pumpkin seeds (also known as pepitas) aren't traditionally the star ingredient, I've featured them more prominently here, using them also as a crust for the tuna.

serves 4

pepita-crusted yellowfin tuna with white bean stew, mole verde, and honey-mustard vinaigrette

1/4 cup vegetable oil

* 4 servings pepita-crusted yellowfin tuna

Kosher salt, to taste

Black pepper, to taste

* 1 1/2 cups white bean stew

* 1 cup mole verde

1 green apple, finely julienned

2 tablespoons cilantro chiffonade

* 1/4 cup honey-mustard vinaigrette

Extra-virgin olive oil, to taste

Sea salt, to taste

★

pepita-crusted yellowfin tuna

Yields 4 servings

1 cup pepitas (see Sources and
  Substitutions)

1/2 cup finely ground panko bread crumbs

1 tablespoon kosher salt

1 tablespoon unsalted butter, melted

1 tablespoon finely chopped flat-leaf
  parsley

1 cup all-purpose flour

5 large eggs

1 pound yellowfin tuna, cut into four
  1/4-pound portions

• In a sauté pan over medium heat, toast
pepitas, constantly tossing, until you can smell
them, about 2 minutes. Set aside to cool.

• In a food processor, combine pepitas,
panko, and salt. Puree until very fine. With
blender running, add butter, then parsley.
Blend until everything is well incorporated
and finely ground.

• To crust tuna, arrange 3 large bowls in a
line. Place flour in first bowl. Whisk eggs in
second bowl. Place pepitas mixture in third
bowl. Drop tuna into flour, shaking bowl
until tuna is completely coated. Remove
tuna from flour, shaking off excess, and
put into bowl with eggs. Shake bowl until
tuna is completely covered in egg. Remove
tuna from egg, shake off excess, and put
into bowl with pepitas. Shake bowl until
tuna is evenly coated. Remove tuna from
pepitas, shake off excess and place on
tray lined with parchment paper.

★

white bean stew

Yields 1 1/2 cups

2 ounces uncooked bacon, diced small

1/2 cup small-diced Spanish onion

2/3 cup dried white beans

12 sprigs thyme, half picked, half tied with
  string

1/2 cup chicken stock (see Basics, p. 268)

1/2 teaspoon kosher salt, to taste

• In a saucepan over low heat, render bacon.
Add onions and sweat over low heat until
translucent. Add white beans, tied thyme
sprigs, and chicken stock. Bring to a boil
over high heat, reduce to a simmer, and
cook until beans are tender, about 1 hour.
Remove thyme sprigs and add thyme leaves
to beans. Season with salt. Stew can be
refrigerated for up to 1 week.

★

mole verde

Yields 1 1/4 cups

1/4 cup pepitas (see Sources and Substitutions)

1/4 teaspoon cumin seeds

1 1/2 cloves

1 cup chopped Spanish onion

1 clove garlic, chopped

1/2 jalapeño chile, chopped

1 tablespoon vegetable oil

1/2 cup chopped tomatillos

3 teaspoons thyme leaves

1 1/2 teaspoons marjoram leaves

1 tablespoon lard

3/4 cup chicken stock (see Basics, p. 268)

1 1/2 tablespoons masa harina (see Sources
  and Substitutions)

2 tablespoons chopped flat-leaf parsley

2 tablespoons lime juice

1 1/2 teaspoons kosher salt

1/4 teaspoon black pepper

• In a sauté pan over medium heat, toss pepitas, cumin, and cloves for 1 minute to toast.

• In a saucepan over medium heat, sauté onions, garlic, and jalapeños in vegetable oil. Add tomatillos and cook for 10 minutes over medium heat. Add thyme, marjoram, cumin, cloves, and pepitas, and cook for 5 more minutes. Pour sauce into a container and set aside.

• In the same saucepan over high heat, melt lard. As soon as it is melted and starts to sizzle, return sauce to the saucepan to refry. Add chicken stock. Reduce heat and bring mixture to a simmer. Cook for 30 minutes. Add masa harina and mix with a hand blender until just slightly chunky. Cook for an additional 10 minutes over low heat until mole starts to thicken.

• Pour into a blender and add parsley and lime juice. Puree until bright green and smooth. Season with salt and pepper. Mole verde can be refrigerated for up to 2 days.

*

honey-mustard vinaigrette

Yields 3/4 cup

1/2 shallot, brunoised

1/2 jalapeño chile, seeded and brunoised

1 tablespoon apple cider vinegar

2 tablespoons Dijon mustard

1/3 cup honey

1/4 cup extra-virgin olive oil

1/2 teaspoon kosher salt

• Thoroughly mix together all of the ingredients. Vinaigrette can be refrigerated for up to 2 days.

putting it all together

• In a cast-iron skillet over medium heat, heat vegetable oil. Season crusted tuna with salt and pepper all over. Place tuna into oil and gently fry on all sides, except the ends, until pepita crust browns slightly, about 1 minute on each side.

• In 2 separate saucepans over medium heat, heat the white bean stew and mole verde.

• Down the middle of each of 4 plates, place a line of white bean stew. Place two 2-tablespoon dots of mole verde in each line of beans. Cut each portion of tuna into 3 even pieces and lay on beans with the centers facing up.

• In a small bowl, toss apple and cilantro with honey-mustard vinaigrette. Place a pile of apple salad between the pieces of tuna. Drizzle tuna with a little extra-virgin olive oil and a sprinkle of sea salt.

Don't be surprised by the number of ingredients
you need to create the pipian crust in this dish. A
long shopping list of herbs, spices, and seeds is
common in Mexican recipes and is one of the reasons
that the cuisine is a source of inspiration in my
cooking. While this Mexican take on pesto tastes
complex, it is actually an easy dish to prepare.
Making the hominy is the most time-consuming step.

serves 4

pipian-crusted black sea bass
with crab pozole verde

* 4 cups crab pozole verde

2 tablespoons vegetable oil

1 pound black sea bass, skin on, cut into four 1/4-pound portions

Kosher salt, to taste

Black pepper, to taste

* 3/4 cup pipian crust

1 tablespoon unsalted butter

1/2 cup julienned radish

1 shallot, shaved thin

3 teaspoons oregano leaves

2 tablespoons extra-virgin olive oil

1 teaspoon lemon juice

*

crab pozole verde

Yields 4 cups

1/4 pound hominy, soaked overnight in water

1/4 pound crab bodies

1/3 cup pepitas (see Sources and
  Substitutions)

2 tomatillos

1 cup chopped Spanish onion

1 jalapeño chile, seeded

1 sprig epazote (see Sources and
  Substitutions)

1 teaspoon lard

1/3 pound serrano ham, diced small

1/4 pound jumbo lump crabmeat

2 tablespoons chopped cilantro

2 tablespoons oregano

1/2 teaspoon kosher salt

• Strain hominy. Add hominy to a saucepan
and cover with water by 1 inch. Bring to a
simmer over low heat and cook for 1 hour.
Wrap crab bodies in cheesecloth and add
to hominy. Simmer over low heat for
another 2 hours, skimming frequently.
(More water may be needed during
cooking.) Remove crab bodies and discard.

• In a food processor, combine pepitas,
tomatillos, onions, jalapeño, epazote, and 2
cups hominy cooking liquid. Puree until
smooth.

• In a sauté pan over high heat, melt lard;
as soon as it starts to sizzle, add puree to
fry. Add serrano ham, reduce heat and
simmer 5 to 8 minutes. Add hominy and fold
in crab, cilantro, and oregano. Season with
salt. Cool.

*

pipian crust

Yields 1 cup

2 tablespoons chopped Spanish onion

4 cloves garlic, chopped

1/2 jalapeño chile, seeded and chopped

1 tablespoon vegetable oil

1 large tomatillo, chopped

Kosher salt, to taste

3 tablespoons pepitas (see Sources and
  Substitutions)

3 tablespoons almond slices

1 tablespoon fennel seeds

1 tablespoon ground cumin

1 tablespoon coriander seeds

3 tablespoons white vinegar

6 tablespoons basil chiffonade

6 tablespoons flat-leaf parsley leaves

9 sprigs cilantro

• Preheat oven to 375°F. In a saucepan over low heat, sweat onion, garlic, and jalapeños in oil until onions are translucent. Add tomatillos and season with salt.

• Place pepitas and almonds on a sheet tray and bake until light golden brown. In a large sauté pan over medium heat, toss fennel, cumin, and coriander for 1 minute to toast.

• Add vinegar, pepitas, almonds, and spices to tomatillo mixture. Cook over low heat until dry.

• In a pot of boiling water, blanch basil 10 seconds, then parsley and cilantro separately, 30 seconds each. Shock herbs in an ice bath.

• In a blender, in 2 batches, combine blanched herbs and tomatillo mixture and puree until bright green and smooth. Taste and adjust seasoning. Pipian crust can be refrigerated for up to 2 days.

putting it all together

• Preheat oven to 400°F. In a saucepan over medium heat, heat crab pozole verde.

• In a cast-iron sauté pan over high heat, heat vegetable oil. Season bass with salt and pepper. Sear skin side until browned. Flip fish over and spread pipian crust onto each piece. Add butter and place the pan in the oven; bake until bass is cooked and pipian starts to brown, about 3 minutes.

• In a small bowl toss radish, shallots, oregano, 1 tablespoon olive oil, and lemon juice. Season with salt and pepper.

• Ladle pozole into 4 shallow bowls, then place bass on top of pozole. Place radish salad on top of the fish then drizzle with remaining extra-virgin olive oil.

In a Spanish kitchen, making flavorful white pil pil sauce is a rite of passage, a difficult task even for a professional cook. Using a blender, as I do in this recipe, is considered cheating, but you'll never be able to taste the difference. The crab and spinach crepe would be out of place in a Spanish kitchen, too, but it is a delicious addition. (NOTE: You'll need to start soaking the cod two days in advance.)

serves 5

cod with crab
and spinach crepes
and pil pil sauce

* 5 crab and spinach crepes

2 tablespoons vegetable oil

1 1/4 pounds black cod, cut into five 1/4-pound portions

Kosher salt, to taste

Black pepper, to taste

2 tablespoons unsalted butter

* 1 cup pil pil sauce

5 cloves roasted garlic (see Basics, p. 267)

2 dried guindilla chiles, cut into rings (see Sources and Substitutions)

2 tablespoons parsley oil (see Basics, p. 267)

*

crab and spinach crepes

Yields 5 crepes

2 large eggs

3/4 cup whole milk

1/2 cup all-purpose flour

1/2 teaspoon kosher salt

2 tablespoons unsalted butter, melted, plus
    10 teaspoons unsalted butter

10 chives, finely minced

1 cup crab and spinach filling (see following
    recipe)

• In a bowl, beat eggs and milk together.
Place flour and salt in a separate bowl.
Add egg mixture to the flour, and mix
thoroughly. Add 2 tablespoons melted
butter and continue to mix. Strain out
lumps using a chinois. Add chives.

• To a 7-inch nonstick pan over low heat,
add 1 teaspoon butter. Once butter has
melted, pour in 3 tablespoons crepe batter
and swirl around, completely coating the
bottom of the pan. Let the pan sit over
heat for 1 minute until the batter releases
itself. Flip the crepe over and cook for 1
additional minute. Remove from the pan
and place on parchment paper. Repeat
cooking process, adding 1 teaspoon butter
and 3 tablespoons batter each time.

• Divide filling among crepes, placing filling
in the middle of each. Fold sides in to form
a square. Place each crepe flap side down
on individual pieces of parchment paper,
top with 1 teaspoon butter, and wrap in
parchment paper.

crab and spinach filling

Yields 1 cup

1/4 Idaho potato, peeled and chopped small

1/2 cup heavy cream

1 sprig rosemary

1 tablespoon vegetable oil

1/2 cup baby spinach

1 clove garlic, minced

3 tablespoons onion confit (see Basics, p. 272)

2 cloves roasted garlic, mashed (see Basics,
    p. 267)

2 ounces jumbo lump crabmeat

1/2 teaspoon kosher salt

• In a saucepan, combine potatoes, cream,
and rosemary. Bring cream to a boil over
high heat. Reduce to a simmer and cook
until potatoes are tender, about 30
minutes. Strain, reserving potatoes and
cream mixture separately.

• In a sauté pan over high heat, heat
vegetable oil and sauté spinach with garlic
until wilted. Drain spinach and chop.

• In a food processor, puree potatoes with
onion confit, roasted garlic, and 1/4 cup
reserved cream mixture. In a bowl, fold
spinach and crab into potato puree.
Season with salt, mix thoroughly and chill.

*

pil pil sauce

Yields 1 cup

2 cloves garlic

1/2 dried guindilla chile, seeds removed (see Sources and Substitutions)

1 sprig rosemary

2 cups extra-virgin olive oil

3 ounces bacalao, soaked in water for 2 days with the water changed twice (see Sources and Substitutions)

1 cup clam stock (see Basics, p. 269)

Kosher salt, to taste

Lemon juice, to taste

• In a saucepan over medium heat, combine garlic, chile, rosemary, and olive oil. Heat mixture to 200°F. Drain bacalao and add to saucepan; cook 8 to 10 minutes. Remove rosemary and discard. Strain mixture, reserving the oil separately from the bacalao, chiles, and garlic. If making ahead, bacalao can be stored in oil in the refrigerator for up to 2 weeks; strain before use.

• In a saucepan, combine bacalao with 2 cups clam stock. Simmer fish until a scum forms on top and the liquid has reduced by half. Do not skim the top; this is the protein from the fish that makes the sauce.

• In a blender, combine fish and stock with reserved chiles and garlic. Puree smooth then pass through a chinois. Do not press any of the solids through; this will cause the sauce to be chunky. Pour the liquid back into blender and slowly add reserved oil to emulsify. You should have a white, silky, smooth sauce. Season with salt and lemon juice. Sauce can be refrigerated for up to 2 days.

putting it all together

• Preheat oven to 400°F. Place the wrapped crepes in the oven for 3 minutes.

• In a cast-iron skillet over high heat, heat vegetable oil. Season fish with salt and pepper. Once pan is hot place the fish in the skillet skin side down; cook until the skin is crisp, about 1 minute, then flip fish over; add butter to the pan, and place in the oven to cook, 3 minutes.

• Remove crepes from the parchment and place 1 on the corner of each of 5 plates. Place a dollop of pil pil sauce on the plate and streak it in a curving motion. Remove the fish from the oven and baste with butter in pan. Then place the fish skin side up on top of the crepe. Garnish each plate with a roasted garlic clove, a few guindilla rings, and a drizzle of parsley oil.

My inspiration for this dish was a Basque-style fisherman's chowder of tuna and potatoes. The dish is almost perfect in its simplicity, but I couldn't resist using it to show off some of Spain's delicious tuna exports: canned Spanish ventresca tuna and salt-cured mojama tuna.

serves 2

tuna four ways

1/4 cup brunoised carrots

1/4 cup brunoised Yukon Gold potatoes

1/4 cup brunoised leeks

1/4 cup brunoised red bell pepper

2 tablespoons vegetable oil

1/2 cup bonito tuna, drained and washed

★ 2 cups marmitako broth

2 tablespoons unsalted butter

2 tablespoons finely chopped flat-leaf parsley

1 tablespoons finely chopped thyme

4 ounces sushi-grade tuna toro, cut into four 1-ounce cubes (keep frozen until just before cooking)

Kosher salt, to taste

★ 1/4 cup migas

6 ounces ventresca tuna (see Sources and Substitutions)

1 ounce mojama, zested (see Sources and Substitutions)

Extra-virgin olive oil, to taste

Coarse sea salt, to taste

*

marmitako broth

Yields 4 cups

1 cup chopped Spanish onion

1/4 carrot, peeled and chopped

1 clove garlic, chopped

1/4 leek, chopped

1/4 cup flat-leaf parsley stems

1 tablespoon extra-virgin olive oil

2 tablespoons choricero chile paste (see Basics, p. 271)

1/2 cup white wine

1/2 pound grill-grade tuna, diced large

4 cups water

1 teaspoon kosher salt

• In a saucepan over low heat, sweat onions, carrots, garlic, leeks, and parsley stems in olive oil until onions are translucent. Add choricero chile paste and cook 5 minutes over low heat. Deglaze pan with wine, and reduce by half. Add tuna and water. Bring to a boil, and then reduce to simmer, skimming the fat frequently. Cook for about 1 hour. Season with salt. Strain through a chinois. Broth can be frozen or refrigerated for up to 1 week.

*

migas

Yields 1/4 cup

2 ounces bacon, chopped

1/4 cup small-diced day-old bread

1 teaspoon finely chopped flat-leaf parsley

1 teaspoon smoked paprika (see Sources and Substitutions)

1/2 teaspoon kosher salt

• In a sauté pan over low heat, render the bacon fat; discard bacon. Add diced bread to the pan and toss over medium heat until toasted. Sprinkle with parsley, smoked paprika, and salt. Lay out on a paper towel to soak up any excess oil.

putting it all together

• In a pot of boiling water, blanch carrots until tender, and shock in ice water. Blanch potatoes until tender, and shock in ice water.

• In a sauté pan over low heat, sweat carrots, leeks, and red bell peppers in vegetable oil. Add potatoes, bonito tuna, and marmitako broth and bring to a boil. Reduce heat and simmer 5 minutes. Stir butter into broth. Add parsley and thyme.

• Place 2 toro cubes on each skewer. Season toro with salt. In a cast iron skillet over high heat, sear cubes on one side until browned.

• Ladle marmitako into 2 bowls. Place seared toro on top of marmitako. Garnish with migas, a few pieces of ventresca tuna, and a shaving of mojama. Drizzle toro with extra-virgin olive oil and a sprinkle of coarse sea salt.

The "linguini" here is not flour and water—it's cut from squid. Pan-seared scallops and cockles give the appearance of a classic Italian frutti di mare, but I serve the dish with an unexpected sweet onion sauce.

serves 2

calamari linguini
with sweet onion cream
and diver scallops

1/2 cup small-diced Spanish onion

1 clove garlic, minced

2 ounces serrano ham, diced small

4 tablespoons vegetable oil

1/4 cup white wine

12 cockles

1/4 cup clam stock (see Basics, p. 269)

1/4 cup English peas

1 cup short fideo pasta (see Sources and Substitutions)

* 3 cups calamari linguini

* 1 cup sweet onion cream

3 tablespoons unsalted butter

2 U/10 diver sea scallops

Kosher salt, to taste

Black pepper, to taste

4 sprigs micro parsley

✳

calamari linguini

Yields 3 cups

1 1/2 pounds calamari
Kosher salt, to taste

• To clean calamari, remove any cartilage from the head, and peel off the skin. Pack cleaned calamari tightly in a rectangular pan. Freeze overnight.

• Remove from freezer, and, using a slicer or mandoline, shave calamari into long strips. Fill a saucepan with water seasoned with salt. Bring salted water to a boil. Blanch calamari strips in boiling water for 30 seconds. Remove and plunge into a salted ice-water bath. Blanched calamari linguini can be frozen for up to 1 week.

✳

sweet onion cream

Yields 1 cup

1 cup heavy cream
1/2 cup onion confit (see Basics, p. 272)
3 cloves roasted garlic (see Basics, p. 267)
Kosher salt, to taste
Black pepper, to taste

• In a saucepan over medium-high heat, reduce heavy cream to 1/2 cup. In a food processor, puree cream, onion confit, and roasted garlic until smooth. Season with salt and pepper.

putting it all together

• Preheat oven to 400°F. In a sauté pan over low heat, sweat onions, garlic, and serrano ham in 3 tablespoons vegetable oil until onion is translucent. Add white wine and cockles; cover and cook until cockles open, 1 to 2 minutes. Remove cockles from shells and return to pan along with clam stock, English peas, and fideo; simmer until fideo is tender, about 3 minutes. Add calamari linguini, sweet onion cream, and 2 tablespoons butter and cook over low heat for 1 minute, stirring constantly to emulsify.

• In the meantime, in a cast-iron skillet over medium heat, heat remaining 1 tablespoon vegetable oil. Season scallops with salt and pepper. Sear scallops on one side. Flip the scallops over and place in oven to cook, 2 minutes. Remove from the oven, add the remaining 1 tablespoon butter, and baste the scallops for 1 minute. Remove from the pan and let scallops rest.

• Spoon the calamari-fideo mix into 2 bowls and top with scallops. Garnish with micro parsley.

I think the best part of this Peruvian seafood chowder (known as chupe) is the egg that is placed on top just before serving. Traditionally, the egg is poached, and when the diner cuts it, the yolk makes a richer sauce for the stew, but the sous vide technique I use makes the whole egg deliciously creamy and custard-like.

serves 2

mixed seafood chowder with purple peruvian potatoes and sous vide eggs

1/4 cup small-diced purple Peruvian potatoes

1 shallot, minced

2 cloves garlic, minced

2 tablespoons vegetable oil

4 mussels

4 cockles

4 langoustines

1/2 cup white wine

1/4 cup bay scallops

1/4 cup calamari rings

1/4 cup small-diced red bell pepper

2 tablespoons cilantro chiffonade

* 2 cups chupe broth

* 2 sous vide eggs

*

sous vide eggs

Yields 2 eggs

2 large eggs

• In a circulator or a saucepan filled with water over medium heat, bring water up to 190°F. Leave a thermometer in the water and maintain a constant temperature. (For further explanation of this technique, see Basics, p. 278.) Place eggs in water and cook for 45 minutes. Remove eggs from the water and place in an ice bath. Reduce water temperature to 122°F. Once the water reaches 122°F, put eggs back into water until needed.

putting it all together

• Bring a pot of water to a boil. Blanch potatoes until tender. Shock potatoes in ice water.

• In a sauté pan over low heat, sweat shallots and garlic in vegetable oil until translucent. Add mussels, cockles, langoustines, and white wine. Cover and cook until mussels and cockles open. Add scallops, calamari, bell peppers, and potatoes and sauté for 1 more minute. Add cilantro, then spoon everything into 2 bowls. In a saucepan over medium heat, heat chupe broth. Peel eggs and place on top of seafood. Serve chupe in a teapot and pour over seafood tableside.

*

chupe broth

Yields 3 cups

1 1/3 cups small-diced Spanish onion

2 cloves garlic, minced

1/4 cup extra-virgin olive oil

2/3 red bell pepper, diced small

2/3 yellow bell pepper, diced small

1 jalapeño chile, seeded and minced

1/2 habanero chile, seeded and minced

1/2 teaspoon minced ginger

1/2 teaspoon ají amarillo chile paste (see Basics, p. 271)

1/2 pound yucca, peeled and diced small

4 cups white shrimp stock (see Basics, p. 270)

1 cup small-diced carrot

1 stalk celery, diced small

1/2 cup heavy cream

• In a saucepan over low heat, sweat onions and garlic in olive oil until onions are translucent. Add bell peppers, chiles, ginger, and chile paste, and sweat over low heat, 15 minutes. Add yucca and shrimp stock and bring to a boil. Add remaining ingredients, bring mixture back to a boil then reduce to a simmer. Continue to cook over low heat until yucca is al dente, about 20 minutes. Pass through a fine-mesh strainer and discard solids. Broth can be frozen for up to 1 week.

In San Sebastian, this baked crab dish, known as txangurro, is served in its shell, topped with bread crumbs. I've refined the presentation, topping the crab salad with a crisp brioche ring and dousing it in a rich sauce. You wouldn't find this buttery addition in Spain, but Americans love the combination of shellfish and butter.

serves 4

dungeness crab gratin
with brioche and donostia sauce

* 2 cups txangurro
* 4 brioche rings
* 1 1/2 cups Donostia sauce

✳

txangurro

Yields 2 cups

1/4 pound jumbo lump Dungeness crabmeat

1/2 red bell pepper, diced small

1/2 green bell pepper, diced small

3 cloves roasted garlic, mashed (see Basics, p. 267)

1/2 cup sauce Basquaise (see Basics, p. 275)

2 tablespoons finely chopped chives

2 tablespoons flat-leaf parsley chiffonade

1 tablespoon extra-virgin olive oil

1/2 teaspoon kosher salt

1/8 teaspoon black pepper

• In a bowl, combine all ingredients and mix well. Txangurro can be refrigerated for up to 2 days.

✳

brioche rings

Yields 4 rings

4 slices brioche, cut into rings with a 1-inch ring mold

2 tablespoons unsalted butter, melted

• Preheat oven to 300°F. Soak brioche in butter and place on a sheet tray. Cook until crisp but not browned, about 5 minutes.

✳

donostia sauce

Yields 1 1/2 cups

2 1/2 pounds lobster bodies, gills and guts removed

4 cups chopped Spanish onion

1 stalk celery, chopped

1/2 bulb baby fennel, chopped

1/2 leek, chopped

2 tablespoons vegetable oil

2 plum tomatoes, chopped

2 tablespoons tomato paste

2 gallons water

1/2 cup unsalted butter

• Preheat oven to 500°F. Put lobster bodies in a roasting pan. Roast bodies until they turn deep red and become very fragrant, about 15 minutes.

• At the same time, in a saucepan over high heat, sauté onions, celery, fennel, and leeks in vegetable oil until vegetables start to caramelize. Add tomatoes and cook for about 15 minutes. Add tomato paste and cook for 5 more minutes. Add lobster bodies, and fill the pan with water. Bring to a boil over high heat. Reduce heat, and simmer for 1 hour. Strain out solids and return liquid to pan. Cook over medium heat to reduce down to 1 cup, skimming the fat as it cooks. Stir in butter when ready to use.

putting it all together

• Preheat oven to 450°F. Fill each of 4 ramekins with 1/2 cup txangurro mixture. Heat in oven, about 3 minutes. Make a small hole in the middle of the txangurro and fill with a brioche ring. Bake 1 more minute to brown the brioche.

• Meanwhile in a saucepan over medium heat, heat Donostia sauce over medium heat. Pour the sauce into a teapot, and serve tableside, pouring the sauce into the middle of the brioche ring until it overflows.

This classic Basque sauce, colored green with parsley, is the key to an otherwise simple fish dish. Be sure to whisk the sauce constantly after you add the butter to get the right consistency. You want it to be just thick enough to coat a spoon.

serves 4

hake with white wine and clam-garlic sauce

1 clove garlic, minced

1 shallot, brunoised

2 tablespoons vegetable oil

20 cockles

1/4 cup white wine

1 cup clam velouté (see Basics, p. 269)

1/4 cup unsalted butter

1/4 cup finely chopped flat-leaf parsley

1 pound hake filet, skin and pin bones removed

Kosher salt, to taste

Black pepper, to taste

2 tablespoons smoked paprika (see Sources and Substitutions)

putting it all together

• Preheat oven to 350°F. In a sauté pan over low heat, sweat garlic and shallots in 1 tablespoon vegetable oil until shallots are translucent. Add cockles and white wine. Cover and cook over high heat until cockles open, about 1 minute. Remove cockles and reserve. Add velouté and bring mixture to a simmer over medium heat. Whisk in butter, stirring constantly to emulsify. Add parsley. Return cockles to sauce.

• At the same time, heat a separate ovenproof sauté pan over high heat with remaining 1 tablespoon vegetable oil. Cut hake into 4 pieces and season with salt and pepper. Sear fish, skin side down, until browned. Flip fish over and place in oven for about 3 minutes.

• Remove fish from the oven and place onto 4 plates. Spoon cockles and sauce onto each plate next to the fish, and pour 1 tablespoon sauce over the fish. Garnish with smoked paprika.

Bobo, a bright orange yucca-saffron sauce, and polenta-like farofa are traditional in Brazilian cooking. Typically this dish is made with shrimp, but I've dressed it up with lobster and added a Caribbean-inspired green papaya salad to bring crunch to the tender dish.

serves 4

maine lobster with bobo sauce, farofa, and green papaya slaw

2 poached Maine lobsters (see Basics, p. 277)

* 3 cups bobo sauce

* 1/2 cup farofa

* 1 cup green papaya slaw

2 tablespoons palm oil (see Sources and Substitutions)

*

bobo sauce

Yields 3 cups

1/2 cup chopped Spanish onion

1 clove garlic, minced

1 tablespoon palm oil (see Sources and
   Substitutions)

1/2 cup peeled, chopped yucca

1/2 teaspoon saffron threads

1 1/4 cups white shrimp stock (see Basics,
   see p. 270)

1/4 cup coconut milk

1/2 teaspoon lime juice

2 tablespoons cilantro chiffonade

• In a saucepan over low heat, sweat onions
and garlic in palm oil until translucent. Add
yucca and saffron, and cook 5 minutes. Add
shrimp stock and cook over medium heat
until yucca is tender, about 20 minutes. Puree
sauce using a hand blender. Stir in coconut
milk and lime juice, and cook an additional 5
minutes. Stir in cilantro. Bobo sauce can be
refrigerated for up to 2 days.

*

farofa

Yields 3/4 cup

1 teaspoon palm oil (see Sources and
   Substitutions)

1/2 cup yucca flour (see Sources and
   Substitutions)

1 tablespoon flat-leaf parsley chiffonade

1 tablespoon cilantro chiffonade

Kosher salt, to taste

• In a sauté pan over medium heat, heat
palm oil. Fold in remaining ingredients and
cook, stirring constantly to avoid sticking
and burning, until the mixture gives off a
toasted aroma, about 5 minutes.

*

green papaya slaw

Yields 1 cup

1 cup cachaça

3/4 cup finely julienned green papaya

2 tablespoons thinly shaved red onion

1/4 habanero chile, seeded and finely
   julienned

2 tablespoons cilantro chiffonade

1/2 tablespoon lime juice

1/4 cup extra-virgin olive oil

Granulated sugar, to taste

Kosher salt, to taste

Black pepper, to taste

• In a saucepan over high heat, bring
cachaça to a boil. Cook off alcohol and
reduce to 1/4 cup. In a bowl, combine with
remaining ingredients. Mix thoroughly.

putting it all together

• Remove meat from lobsters. Slice tails
into twelve 1/4-inch-thick rounds and chop
knuckle meat. Leave claw meat whole.

• In a saucepan over medium heat, combine
knuckle meat and bobo sauce. When hot,
add tail slices and claw meat, just to coat.

• In a separate saucepan over low heat,
heat farofa.

• Place 3 tail slices and a claw on each of 4
plates. Pour 1 tablespoon bobo sauce over
each piece of lobster, making sure to get
some of the knuckle meat. Spoon 2 tablespoons
farofa in a line at the bottom of each plate.
Top each piece of lobster with papaya slaw.
Drizzle each plate with palm oil.

Everybody loves mashed potatoes, which makes
Peruvian causa—mashed potato cakes—a great
basis for experimenting with Spanish flavors. Here
I've added saffron to the potato cakes, and
balanced the pretty layered dish with a slightly
vinegary carrot escabeche.

serves 2

terrine of dungeness crab
and saffron potato
with carrot escabeche

1/2 cup micro cilantro

1 teaspoon extra-virgin olive oil

1/2 teaspoon lemon juice

Kosher salt, to taste

* 2 cups saffron-potato puree

* 1 cup crab mixture

* 1 cup carrot escabeche

2 tablespoons parsley oil (see Basics, p. 267)

*

saffron-potato puree

Yields 2 cups

1 1/2 russet potatoes, peeled and chopped
1 tablespoon saffron threads
1/4 cup extra-virgin olive oil
Kosher salt, to taste
Black pepper, to taste

• Fill a saucepan with water. Add saffron and potatoes and bring to a boil over high heat. Cook until potatoes are tender. Strain potatoes and pass through a tamis into a bowl. Mix potatoes with olive oil, salt, and pepper until silky smooth. Store at room temperature until ready to serve.

*

crab mixture

Yields 1 cup

1/3 pound Dungeness crabmeat
4 cloves roasted garlic (see Basics, p. 267)
1 1/2 tablespoons crème fraîche
1 tablespoon lemon juice
1 1/2 tablespoons minced chives
1 1/2 tablespoons mayonnaise
Kosher salt, to taste

• In a bowl, combine all ingredients. Mix thoroughly.

*

carrot escabeche

Yields 2 cups

1/2 carrot, cut into ribbons
1 shallot, thinly sliced
5 teaspoons thyme leaves
1 tablespoon honey
1/4 cup white wine vinegar
1/3 cup extra-virgin olive oil
1/2 teaspoon granulated sugar
1/2 teaspoon kosher salt
1/4 teaspoon black pepper

• In a bowl, combine all ingredients. Mix thoroughly.

putting it all together

• In a bowl, toss micro cilantro with extra-virgin olive oil, lemon juice, and salt.

• Place a 3-inch-square mold in the middle of each of 2 plates and fill with 1/2 inch saffron-potato puree. Pack the crab mixture on top, 1 inch deep, and then finish with another 1/2-inch layer of saffron-potato puree. Remove molds. Top terrines with cilantro salad. Place 3 small piles carrot escabeche around each plate, and place 3 dots of parsley oil among the piles.

Baked clams and rice is a simple Basque dish—until you add high-quality ingredients. I always use bomba rice, a risotto-style short-grain rice that keeps its shape when cooked, adding texture to the dish. It is more expensive than other rice, but it is almost impossible to overcook. (NOTE: This recipe requires a whipped cream charger.)

serves 2

littleneck clams
with bomba rice, artichoke confit, and parmesan espuma

1 cup small-diced Spanish onion

3 cloves garlic, minced

1 tablespoon vegetable oil

8 littleneck clams

1/2 cup white wine

* 2 cups cooked bomba rice

1/2 cup chopped, cooked clams, reserved from clam stock (see Basics, p. 269)

1 tablespoon unsalted butter

2 tablespoons chopped flat-leaf parsley

6 slices confit artichoke (see Basics, p. 271)

* 1/4 cup parmesan espuma

1 lemon, zested

*

bomba rice

Yields 2 cups

1/4 cup small-diced Spanish onion

2 cloves roasted garlic, mashed (see Basics,
   p. 267)

2 tablespoons vegetable oil

1 cup uncooked bomba rice (see Sources
   and Substitutions)

1 1/2 cups clam stock (see Basics, p. 269)

Kosher salt, to taste

• Preheat oven to 325°F. In an ovenproof saucepan over low heat, sweat onions and garlic in vegetable oil until onions are translucent. Add rice and stir to coat. Add clam stock and season with salt. Bring mixture to a boil over high heat. Remove from heat. Cover pan tightly and bake 18 minutes. Pour rice onto a tray and fluff with a fork.

*

parmesan espuma

Yields about 2 cups

1 cup heavy cream

3 cloves roasted garlic (see Basics, p. 267)

Kosher salt, to taste

3 ounces parmesan cheese, grated

1 sheet gelatin

• In a saucepan over medium heat, combine cream and garlic. Season with salt. Reduce cream mixture by half. Whisk in parmesan and continue to cook over low heat until cheese melts. Bloom gelatin in ice water. Squeeze out any excess water and whisk gelatin into the cream. Pass mixture through a chinois. Mixture can be refrigerated for up to 2 days. When ready to use, fill a whipped cream charger halfway with mixture and charge with 2 nitrous canisters. Place the charger in a warm place until use. (Do not charge more than 3 hours in advance.)

putting it all together

• In a sauté pan over low heat, sweat onions and garlic in oil until onions are translucent. Add littleneck clams and wine. Cover pan and cook over high heat until the clams have opened, 1 to 2 minutes. Add rice and chopped clams (reserved from clam stock) to the sauté pan. Stir in butter and parsley.

• Spoon rice into a line on each of 2 plates. Top rice with 4 littleneck clams in a line, with confit artichoke slices placed in between them. Squeeze out a line of parmesan espuma next to the rice. Garnish with lemon zest.

Is this dish Spanish? Or is it French? On my most recent trip to Bayonne in Basque country, I realized that I shouldn't try to answer that question; I should just eat. Moules frites is a French classic, but the tomato-based sauce Basquaise, with the addition of chorizo, is a spicy, Spanish touch.

serves 2

blue bay mussels
with potato batons
and lemon aïoli

16 cups clam stock (see Basics, p. 269)

30 blue bay mussels

1/2 cup small-diced chorizo de Bilbao

8 cups vegetable oil (reserved from potato batons) for frying, plus 2 teaspoons for sautéing

6 tablespoons brunoised Spanish onion

1 clove garlic, minced

2 tablespoons brunoised red bell pepper

2 tablespoons brunoised green bell pepper

3 cups sauce Basquaise (see Basics, p. 275)

* 2 cups potato batons

Kosher salt, to taste

1 teaspoon espelette powder (see Sources and Substitutions)

2 tablespoons flat-leaf parsley chiffonade

* 1/4 cup lemon aioli

*

potato batons

Yields 2 cups

8 cups vegetable oil, for frying

1 Idaho potato

• In a fryer or a deep, heavy-bottomed 4-quart pan, heat vegetable oil to 275°F. Peel potato, cut down to a 3-inch-long rectangle, and then cut into fries. Blanch potatoes in the fryer until soft, about 3 minutes. Set aside until ready to serve. Reserve frying oil.

*

lemon aïoli

Yields 1/2 cup

1/2 cup vegetable oil

2 lemons, zested

1 teaspoon turmeric

1 large egg yolk

1 clove roasted garlic (see Basics, p. 267)

1/2 teaspoon kosher salt

1 tablespoon lemon juice

• In a saucepan over low heat, warm vegetable oil. Add lemon zest and allow to cook, about 15 minutes. Stir in turmeric. Strain mixture through a chinois, and place lemon oil in the refrigerator to cool.

• In a food processor, combine egg yolk, roasted garlic, salt, and lemon juice. Puree until smooth. While processing, slowly add lemon oil until the mixture forms a mayonnaise-like consistency. Taste and adjust seasoning. Aïoli can be refrigerated for up to 1 week; refresh with fresh lemon juice before using.

putting it all together

• Bring 15 3/4 cups clam stock to a boil. Add mussels and cook until just opened, about 1 minute. Remove mussels from shells.

• In a saucepan over low heat, render chorizo in 2 teaspoons vegetable oil for about 1 minute. Add onions, garlic, and peppers, and gently sauté over medium heat until onions and peppers are soft. Add sauce Basquaise, mussels, and 1/4 cup clam stock. Bring to a simmer over medium heat.

• In a fryer or deep, heavy-bottomed 4-quart pan, heat vegetable oil reserved from potato batons to 375°F. Add potato batons and fry until golden brown. In a large bowl, toss potato batons with salt, espelette powder, and parsley.

• Fill the bottom of 2 small ramekins with lemon aïoli and stand potato batons on end in the ramekins. Fill 2 small Dutch ovens or small lidded bowls with the mussels; cover and serve.

Although it doesn't look like it, all the elements of a classic red snapper a la Veracruzana are here— except the red snapper. Instead I've used wild turbot, the best light, firm-fleshed fish available. And I've broken down the Veracruzana sauce to focus on its most important flavors: tomatoes, olives, capers, and jalapeño chiles.

serves 4

turbot a la veracruzana with olive-caper puree, jalapeño paint, and sea foam

1 pound turbot filet, cut into four 1/4-pound portions

Kosher salt, to taste

Black pepper, to taste

2 1/4 cups vegetable oil

1 tablespoon unsalted butter

12 capers, drained

* 1/4 cup jalapeño paint

12 confit cherry tomatoes (see Basics, p. 272)

* 1/2 cup olive-caper puree

* 1/2 cup sea foam

2 teaspoons thyme leaves

4 Manzanilla olives, sliced thin

*

jalapeño paint

Yields 1/4 cup

3 tablespoons chopped chives

3/4 cup flat-leaf parsley leaves

1/4 cup baby spinach

5 jalapeño chiles, seeded

2 scallions, green parts only

1 teaspoon kosher salt

1/4 teaspoon xanthan gum (see Sources and Substitutions)

• In a pot of boiling water, blanch chives and parsley for 30 seconds, and blanch baby spinach for 10 seconds. Shock herbs and spinach in ice water when done. In a blender, combine chives, parsley, spinach, jalapeños, scallions, and salt. Puree, adding ice as needed to achieve a smooth, loose consistency. Add xanthan gum and puree.

*

olive-caper puree

Yields 3/4 cup

1/3 cup green Spanish olives, pitted

1 teaspoon caper nonpareils

2 tablespoons rosemary oil (see Basics, p. 268)

1 tablespoon sherry vinegar

1 tablespoon dried thyme

1/2 tablespoon lemon juice

1/4 cup extra-virgin olive oil

• In a blender, combine all ingredients except olive oil. Puree until smooth. While processing, add olive oil to emulsify. Pass through a tamis. Puree can be refrigerated for up to 2 days.

*

sea foam

Yields about 2 cups

1 cup oyster juice

1 tablespoon soy lecithin (see Sources and Substitutions)

• Combine oyster juice and soy lecithin. Stir until the lecithin dissolves. Using a hand blender, froth sea foam. Use immediately.

putting it all together

• Season turbot with salt and pepper. In a cast-iron skillet over high heat, heat 1/4 cup vegetable oil. Once hot, place fish in the pan and add butter. Sear for 1 minute. Flip fish over and cook for 1 additional minute.

• In a fryer or deep, heavy-bottomed 4-quart pan, heat 2 cups vegetable oil to 400°F. Add capers and fry until crispy, about 30 seconds. Lay out on paper towels to drain.

• Using a paintbrush, paint a line of the jalapeño paint onto 4 plates. Place 3 confit tomatoes in a line on top of each streak of paint. In a corner of each plate, place a dollop of olive-caper puree and slightly streak the puree in the corner. Place the turbot just above the jalapeño paint. Place 2 tablespoons sea foam on top of each piece of turbot. Garnish the plate with thyme leaves, slivered olives, and fried capers.

In Mexico, flavorful fishes and sauces—such as the classic garlic-lime mojo de ajo made in the final step of this recipe—are typically paired with boring white rice. These potato cakes are my alternative. Made with parsley, cilantro, basil, chives, and plenty of poblano chiles, these crisped cakes are far from bland.

serves 4

king salmon al mojo de ajo with poblano-potato cakes and fava bean salpicon

1 pound king salmon, cut into four 1/4-pound portions

2 teaspoons kosher salt, plus more to taste

1 teaspoon black pepper, plus more to taste

2 tablespoons vegetable oil

1/2 cup all-purpose flour

* 4 poblano-potato cakes

1/2 cup plus 1/2 teaspoon lime juice

1/4 cup garlic chips (see Basics, p. 272)

6 tablespoons unsalted butter

2 tablespoons finely chopped flat-leaf parsley

2 tablespoons micro cilantro

1 teaspoon extra-virgin olive oil

* 1 1/2 cups fava bean salpicon

*

poblano-potato cakes

Yields 4 cakes

1/2 pound Idaho potatoes, peeled and chopped

1 large hard-boiled egg

1 teaspoon basil chiffonade

1 teaspoon chopped cilantro

1 teaspoon chopped chives

2 tablespoons flat-leaf parsley chiffonade

1 roasted poblano chile, chopped (see
   Basics, p. 273)

1 teaspoon kosher salt

Black pepper, to taste

• To a saucepan, add potatoes and enough
water to cover; bring to a boil and cook
until tender. Pass potatoes through a food
mill along with hard-boiled egg.

• In a pot of boiling water, blanch basil for
10 seconds, then cilantro, chives, and parsley
separately, 30 seconds each. Shock herbs in
ice water. In a blender, combine blanched
herbs and enough water to puree smooth,
about 1 tablespoon.

• In a bowl, mix together the potato mixture,
herb puree, poblanos, salt, and pepper.
Spread out on a baking tray to cool and
firm. When cool, form into 4 oval cakes. Lay
on parchment paper, cover with plastic
wrap, and refrigerate.

*

fava bean salpicon

Yields 1 1/2 cups

1/2 cup fava beans

1/2 cup seeded and small-diced plum
   tomatoes

1/4 cup small-diced red onion

1/4 cup cilantro chiffonade

1/4 cup lime juice

1/4 cup extra-virgin olive oil

1/2 teaspoon kosher salt

• Bring a pot of water to a boil. Blanch
fava beans for 45 seconds. Shock in ice
water. In a bowl, mix all ingredients and
refrigerate until ready to serve.

putting it all together

• Preheat oven to 350°F. Season salmon with
salt and pepper. In a cast-iron skillet over
high heat, heat 1 tablespoon vegetable oil.
Place salmon in skillet flesh side down and
cook until browned. Flip salmon over and
place in oven for 3 minutes or until cooked
to desired doneness.

• Meanwhile, in a sauté pan over high heat,
heat remaining 1 tablespoon vegetable oil.
In a bowl, combine flour, 2 teaspoons salt,
and 1 teaspoon pepper. Dredge poblano-
potato cakes in mixture and brown in the
hot pan, about 1 minute per side.

• At the same time, make mojo de ajo. In a
saucepan, combine 1/2 cup lime juice and
the garlic chips, and bring to a boil. Remove
from heat and whisk in 4 tablespoons
butter slowly so the sauce doesn't break.
Add parsley and season with salt to taste.

• In a bowl, toss micro cilantro with olive oil,
1/2 teaspoon lime juice, and salt to taste.

• Place a poblano-potato cake on each of
4 plates. Remove fish from oven and baste
with remaining 2 tablespoons butter. Place
salmon piece on top of each potato cake,
and pour mojo de ajo over salmon. Arrange
the fava bean salpicon around the salmon.
Top salmon with cilantro salad.

aves y
carnes
poultry & meat

In Peru, ají de gallina, a spicy shredded chicken stew, is a warm, homey, winter meal. I wanted to recreate its unique flavors—the secret is the apricot-scented ají mirasol chile—but I've refined the cooking technique. Here I use squab. Cooking it sous vide improves the texture, so I don't shred the breast meat—it's too good just the way it is.

serves 2

sous vide squab
with ají gallina sauce

1/4 cup walnuts

10 pitted black olives

* 2 servings sous vide squab

1 tablespoon extra-virgin olive oil

Kosher salt, to taste

Black pepper, to taste

* 1/2 cup ají gallina sauce

12 slices confit purple Peruvian potatoes (see Basics, p. 272)

1/4 cup caramelized red pearl onions (see Basics, p. 271)

Tol

ste

hea

bea

add

fas

bra

twis

and

serve

sou

wit

and

★ 2 cup

★ 1/2 cu

★ 2 ser

1 oun

2 oun

1/4 cu

1 tab

*

braised cabbage

Yields 1/2 cup

1 cup thinly sliced Spanish onion

1 clove garlic, minced

1 tablespoon vegetable oil

2 cups shaved green cabbage

1/4 cup chicken stock (see Basics, p. 268)

2 tablespoons white vinegar

2 tablespoons honey

1/2 teaspoon granulated sugar

Kosher salt, to taste

• In a saucepan over medium heat, sauté onions and garlic in oil until onions are translucent. Add cabbage and sauté over high heat until slightly colored. Add stock and cook over medium heat 15 minutes. Add vinegar, honey, and sugar. Season with salt. Cook 10 minutes over medium heat. Strain any excess juice. Place cabbage in refrigerator to cool. Braised cabbage can be refrigerated for up to 2 days.

*

black bean stew

Yields 2 cups

3 ounces dried alubias black beans

1/2 roasted green bell pepper (see Basics, p. 273)

1/3 cup onion confit (see Basics, p. 272)

1/4 pound chorizo, diced small

2 cloves garlic

2 teaspoons thyme leaves

2 bay leaves

3 cups chicken stock (see Basics, p. 268)

• Soak beans in water, 24 hours. In a blender, puree roasted pepper and onion confit. In a saucepan over low heat, render chorizo. Add garlic and sweat until translucent. Drain and rinse beans. Add beans, thyme, and bay leaves to pan. Cover with stock and cook over medium heat until beans are tender, about 3 hours. Add roasted pepper puree and continue cooking for 15 minutes. Remove bay leaves. Black bean stew can be refrigerated for up to 1 week.

*

sous vide or braised pork belly

Yields 2 servings

to brine pork belly:

1/2 cup apple cider vinegar

2 tablespoons honey

2 tablespoons molasses

1/2 cup soy sauce

2 cups water

1 stick canela (see Sources and Substitutions)

1 star anise

1 tablespoon pickling spice

1 teaspoon red pepper flakes

2 tablespoons kosher salt

2 tablespoons granulated sugar

6 ounces pork belly, skin removed

For braising method only:

2 tablespoons vegetable oil

1 cup chopped Spanish onion

1/4 carrot, chopped

2 cloves garlic

1 cup sherry

4 cups chicken stock (see Basics, p. 268)

• To brine pork belly: In a bowl, combine apple cider vinegar, honey, molasses, soy sauce, water, spices, and sugar. Mix well until salt and sugar have dissolved. Combine pork belly and brine and refrigerate, 2 days.

• For sous vide method: Remove pork from brine and cut into 2 even pieces; place into a sealable bag along with 2 cups brining liquid. Close bag and squeeze out as much air as possible. (A vacuum sealer works best.) In a circulator or pan filled with water over low heat, bring water to 145°F. Keep thermometer in water and maintain a constant temperature. (For further explanation of this technique, see Basics, p. 278.) Place the bag containing the pork into the water and cover to reduce evaporation. Cook 24 hours.

• Alternatively, to make braised pork belly: Preheat oven to 250°F. Remove pork from brine and rinse; cut into 2 pieces. In a braising pan over high heat, sear pork on all sides in vegetable oil. Remove pork. In same pan, combine onions, carrots, and garlic. Caramelize the vegetables over high heat. Deglaze saucepan with sherry, scraping the bottom of the pan, and reduce mixture to a syrup. Place pork back into saucepan and add stock to cover. Bring stock to a boil. Remove from heat, cover, and bake 6 1/2 hours.

putting it all together

• In a saucepan over medium heat, heat black bean stew. In a separate saucepan over medium heat, heat braised cabbage.

• In a sauté pan over high heat, sear pork belly, morcilla sausage, and chorizo. Place morcilla in the bottom of 2 small Dutch ovens or small bowls with lids. Fill each with beans. Top each with a piece of pork belly, chorizo, and braised cabbage. Garnish with pickled guindilla chiles and parsley.

The American tradition of barbecue has its roots in Mexican barbacoa, an ancient method of cooking a whole animal in a pit over a smoldering flame. The result is lush meat that tastes as though it has been steamed, roasted, and smoked. When I don't have the time or space—or appetite—to cook a whole lamb, I use this method to achieve the same complex flavors.

serves 4

slow-cooked lamb shoulder with papas y chorizo and avocado mousse

* 3 cups papas y chorizo

* 4 servings braised lamb

   1/4 cup purslane chiffonade

   2 tablespoons extra-virgin olive oil

   Kosher salt, to taste

* 1/2 cup avocado mousse

*

papas y chorizo

Yields 3 cups

4 cups vegetable oil, for frying

3 Yukon Gold potatoes, diced small

3 ounces chorizo, minced

2 tablespoons extra-virgin olive oil

1 cup small-diced Spanish onion

2 cloves garlic, minced

2 tablespoons adobo marinade (see Basics, p. 274)

1 roasted poblano chile, sliced (see Basics, p. 273)

1 tablespoon cilantro chiffonade

• In a fryer or deep, heavy-bottomed 2-quart pan, heat vegetable oil to 275°F. Add potatoes and cook until tender.

• In a sauté pan over low heat, render chorizo in olive oil. Add onions and garlic and sweat over low heat until translucent. Add adobo marinade, roasted poblanos, and potatoes and cook over low heat 10 minutes. Fold in cilantro.

*

braised lamb

Yields 4 servings

4 cups vegetable oil, for frying, plus 2 tablespoons

3 guajillo chiles, seeded (see Sources and Substitutions)

1/2 teaspoon ground cumin

1 clove

2 whole allspice berries

1 tablespoon dried Mexican oregano (see Sources and Substitutions)

7 teaspoons thyme leaves

2 cloves garlic

1/2 cup small-diced Spanish onion

1 tablespoon apple cider vinegar

1 teaspoon kosher salt, plus more to taste

1 teaspoon black pepper, plus more to taste

3/4 pound lamb shoulder

5 avocado leaves (see Sources and Substitutions)

2 banana leaves (see Sources and Substitutions)

1/3 cup chicken stock (see Basics, p. 268)

2 cups canned chopped tomatoes

2 1/2 teaspoons cilantro leaves

*

avocado mousse

Yields 1/2 cup

1/3 avocado

1/4 jalapeño chile, chopped

2 1/2 teaspoons cilantro leaves

1 tablespoon whole milk

1/4 cup heavy cream

1/4 teaspoon kosher salt

Granulated sugar, to taste

• In a blender, combine avocado, jalapeño, and cilantro. Puree until smooth. While processing, add milk and cream. Season with salt and sugar. Cool in refrigerator for about 10 minutes. Use immediately.

---

putting it all together

• In a sauté pan over medium heat, heat papas y chorizo. In a saucepan over medium heat, heat lamb and sauce.

• In a bowl, toss purslane in olive oil and kosher salt.

• Fill four 4-inch casserole dishes with 1/2 inch papas y chorizo casserole. Remove lamb from sauce and place on top of papas y chorizo in the shape of a cone. Drizzle with sauce. Form 4 quenelles out of avocado mousse and place 1 on each plate next to the lamb. Garnish with purslane salad.

• Preheat oven to 275°F. In a fryer or deep, heavy-bottomed 2-quart pan, heat 4 cups vegetable oil to 375°F. Drop guajillo chiles in the fryer for 10 seconds and then put them in a container of cold water to soak.

• In a sauté pan over medium heat, toss cumin, clove, and allspice for 1 minute to toast.

• In a blender, combine guajillos with a 1/4 cup soaking water, cumin, clove, allspice, oregano, 3 teaspoons thyme, garlic, onions, and vinegar. Season with salt and pepper to taste. Puree until smooth. Set aside 1/2 cup of paste and rub the remaining paste on lamb shoulder.

• Wrap lamb with avocado leaves and then in banana leaves. Place on a baking rack in a baking pan and add water to cover bottom of pan. Cover lamb with foil. Cook until tender, 3 to 4 hours.

• Allow lamb to cool, then cut meat into strips. Place lamb in a braising pan and sauté in remaining 2 tablespoons vegetable oil over high heat until browned. Add in reserved chile paste, stock, and tomatoes, and cook over medium-low heat until liquid thickens. Season with 1 teaspoon salt and 1 teaspoon pepper. Add remaining thyme and cilantro.

The adobo marinade in this carne asada is a Mexican creation, but it is the perfect addition to an all-American cookout. You can prepare these steaks in the oven, but cooking them on a hot grill will add another layer of flavor. I repeatedly baste the sirloins while grilling to create a thin, spicy crust on the meat.

serves 4

grilled sirloin
with arroz con crema
and tomatillo escabeche

* 2 1/2 cups arroz con crema
* 4 servings marinated sirloin steaks
  Kosher salt, to taste
  Black pepper, to taste
* 2 cups tomatillo escabeche

*

arroz con crema

Yields 2 1/2 cups

1 cup whole milk

1/2 cup plus 2 1/2 tablespoons heavy cream

2 cups cooked long grain rice

3/4 cup roasted corn kernels (see Basics, p. 273)

1/2 cup small-diced roasted poblano chiles (see Basics, p. 273)

3 ounces Chihuahua cheese, grated (about 2 cups)

1 ounce queso fresco cheese, crumbled

1/2 cup plus 2 1/2 tablespoons crema Mexicana (see Basics, p. 274)

Kosher salt, to taste

• In a saucepan, combine milk and cream and bring to a boil over high heat. Reduce heat to low, add rice, corn, and poblanos and simmer for about 2 minutes. Fold in Chihuahua cheese, queso fresco, and crema Mexicana. Taste and adjust seasoning. Arroz con crema can be refrigerated for up to 2 days.

*

marinated sirloin steaks

Yields 4 servings

4 (6-ounce) portions 21-day dry-aged sirloin steak

2 cups adobo marinade (see Basics, p. 274)

• Coat steaks with marinade and allow to sit for at least 2 hours. Reserve marinade for basting.

*

tomatillo escabeche

Yields 2 cups

12 tomatillos, sliced 1/8 inch thick

3 shallots, shaved

3 jalapeño chiles, seeded and brunoised

1/4 cup cilantro chiffonade

1/4 cup lime juice

1/4 cup extra-virgin olive oil

1/2 teaspoon granulated sugar

1/2 teaspoon kosher salt

Black pepper, to taste

• In a bowl, combine all ingredients. Mix well.

putting it all together

• In a saucepan over low heat, heat arroz con crema. Season steaks with salt and pepper. Grill over high heat, basting repeatedly, to desired doneness, about 4 minutes for medium-rare. Remove steaks from the grill and allow to rest for at least 2 minutes.

• Divide arroz con crema among 4 shallow bowls. Slice steaks and lay in shingles on top of arroz con crema. Layer tomatillo escabeche on top of steak by placing down a few tomatillos and then some of the jalapeño, shallot, and cilantro. Add another layer of tomatillos then more of the jalapeño, shallot, and cilantro, and finally another layer of tomatillos.

I found the inspiration for this decadent dish while working the kitchens of New York's Rainbow Room. At the time, the menu included a very traditional version of tournedos Rossini, a classic French dish that pairs foie gras and beef. I tweaked the traditional, caramelizing the foie gras and adding some Spanish elements, both creamy and acidic, to round out the dish.

serves 2

filet mignon
with caramelized foie gras torchon
and cabrales demi-glace

2 (1/4-pound) filets mignons

Kosher salt, to taste

Black pepper, to taste

1 tablespoon vegetable oil

2 tablespoons unsalted butter

✽ 1 cup demi-glace

2 1/2 ounces Cabrales cheese

2 (1/4-inch) slices foie gras torchon (see Basics, see p. 276)

1 tablespoon turbinado sugar

2 tablespoons parsley oil (see Basics, p. 267)

*

demi-glace

Yields 4 cups

5 pounds veal bones

8 cups chopped Spanish onions

1 carrot, chopped

2 stalks celery, chopped

4 beefsteak tomatoes, chopped

1/2 cup tomato paste

4 gallons water

4 cups red wine

• Preheat oven to 500°F. Place bones in a roasting pan. Roast bones until they get a nice dark brown color, about 30 minutes. Remove bones from the pan and place in a stock pot.

• Move the roasting pan to the top of the stove over high heat. Add onions, carrots, and celery and cook, stirring constantly, until the bottom of the pan is clean. (The liquid in the vegetables will deglaze the pan.) Add tomatoes and cook 15 minutes, again stirring constantly so the mixture doesn't burn. Add tomato paste and cook 5 minutes.

• Add vegetables to the pot with the bones and fill with water. Bring water to a boil over high heat. Reduce heat and simmer for 5 hours, skimming all the fat off the top as it cooks. Strain out solids and return all the liquid to the pot. Over high heat, reduce to 4 cups.

• In a separate saucepan over hight heat, reduce wine to a syrup then pour into demi-glace. Place in the refrigerator to cool. The demi-glace will solidify as it cools. Demi-glace can be frozen for up to 1 month.

putting it all together

• Preheat oven to 400°F. Season filets with salt and pepper. In a cast-iron skillet over high heat, heat vegetable oil. Place filets into the pan and sear on one side. Flip the filets over and place in the oven until they reach the desired doneness. Remove filets from the oven, add 1 tablespoon butter to the pan and baste filets.

• At the same time, in a saucepan over medium heat, heat demi-glace. When demi-glace is hot, whisk in 2 ounces Cabrales cheese and 1 tablespoon butter.

• Place a filet in the middle of each plate and then spoon 2 tablespoons Cabrales demi-glace over each filet. Sprinkle one side of the torchon slices with the sugar. Using a blowtorch brûlée the torchons and place them atop the filets. (If you don't have a blowtorch eliminate the sugar and this step.) Around the plate, place a few crumbles of Cabrales and drizzle parsley oil.

This recipe is inspired not by traditional Spanish recipes, but by modern Spanish chefs, who are using cooking techniques and flavors in unexpected ways. I started with an American comfort-food dish—French toast—and added surprising Spanish flavors such as smoked paprika and sherry. The foie gras is a rich addition to this already-decadent dish, but the orange marmalade lightens it up.

serves 2

foie gras and seville orange marmalade on french toast

1/2 pound foie gras, cut into 2 pieces, each less than 1 inch thick

Kosher salt, to taste

Black pepper, to taste

2 pieces brioche, crust removed, cut into 2-inch-by-4-inch-by-1-inch rectangles

* 2 cups French toast batter

1 tablespoon unsalted butter

* 2 tablespoons Seville orange marmalade

* 2 tablespoons honey crème fraîche

* 1 tablespoon sherry reduction

Extra-virgin olive oil, to taste

Sea salt, to taste

✳

french toast batter

Yields 2 cups

3 large eggs

3/4 cup whole milk

3/4 cup heavy cream

1 tablespoon ground cinnamon

1 teaspoon nutmeg

1/2 cup granulated sugar

1 teaspoon smoked paprika (see Sources and Substitutions)

• In a bowl, combine all ingredients. Using a hand blender, puree until smooth. Chill.

✳

seville orange marmalade

Yields 3/4 cup

1 shallot, brunoised

1/2 cup small-diced dried peaches

1/2 tablespoon vegetable oil

1/2 navel orange, juiced

3 Seville oranges, segmented and zested

1 clove

1/4 stick cinnamon

1 star anise

2 tablespoons granulated sugar

1 tablespoon honey

1 tablespoon white wine vinegar

1/2 teaspoon extra-virgin olive oil

• In a saucepan over low heat, sweat shallots and dried peaches in oil until the peaches are very soft. Add orange juice and zest and continue to cook.

• In a separate sauté pan over medium heat, toss the spices for 1 minute to toast. Grind spices.

• Add spices, sugar, and honey to dried-peach mixture. Cook over low heat until almost all of the liquid is gone. Fold in orange segments, vinegar, and olive oil. Spread the mixture on a tray and refrigerate. The mixture will thicken as it cools. Marmalade can be refrigerated for up to 1 week.

*

honey crème fraîche

Yields 2 tablespoons

2 tablespoons crème fraîche

1/2 teaspoon honey

Kosher salt, to taste

• In a bowl, whisk crème fraîche and honey. The crème fraîche will loosen once you add the honey, so whisk until it starts to stiffen up again. Season with salt and chill. Honey crème fraîche can be refrigerated for up to 1 week.

*

sherry reduction

Yields 1/4 cup

1 star anise

2 cloves

1 cup dry sherry

2 tablespoons honey

2 tablespoons glucose syrup (see Sources and Substitutions)

• In a saucepan over medium heat, toast spices for 1 minute. Remove pan from heat and add sherry. Return pan to heat and raise to high. Cook until sherry is reduced to 1/4 cup. Whisk in honey and glucose syrup. Reduce to 1/4 cup. Strain through a chinois. Sherry reduction can be refrigerated for up to 1 month.

putting it all together

• Preheat oven to 350°F. Place a cast-iron pan over medium-high heat. Lightly score one side of each piece of foie gras and season with salt and pepper. Once the pan is hot, place the foie gras in the pan, scored side down. Place pan in the oven to cook, 1 minute. Remove pan and flip foie gras. The foie gras should have a nice brown sear with even score marks. Place the pan back on the burner over medium heat until the second side is seared. Press on the middle of the foie gras to test doneness. It should be slightly firm but tender. If not yet firm, return pan to the oven for a few seconds to finish.

• Soak brioche in French toast batter for 1 minute. In a large sauté pan over medium heat, melt butter. Brown the soaked brioche on all sides until golden brown.

• On each of 2 plates put a small dot of marmalade right in the middle and place the brioche on top so that it won't slide around. Place a piece of foie gras on top of each brioche. In the corner of each plate, place a dot of honey crème fraîche, and in the opposite corner, place a quenelle of marmalade. Drizzle foie gras with sherry reduction and a little extra-virgin olive oil and sprinkle it with sea salt.

This is my take on the dish lomo saltado. Think of it as a Peruvian stir-fry. The traditional ingredients are typical of South America—meat, potatoes, onions, tomatoes, peppers—but the technique comes from the region's Chinese immigrants.

serves 4

kobe beef tenderloin with papas al ajillo, caramelized cipollini onions, and roasted red pepper puree

8 cups vegetable oil (reserved from papas al ajillo) for frying, plus 2 tablespoons for searing

* 4 servings papas al ajillo

3 cloves garlic, minced

1 tablespoon flat-leaf parsley chiffonade

2 tablespoons extra-virgin olive oil

Kosher salt, to taste

* 4 servings black pepper–rubbed beef tenderloin

4 caramelized cipollini onions (see Basics, p. 271)

4 confit cherry tomatoes (see Basics, p. 272)

* 1/4 cup roasted red pepper puree

*

papas al ajillo

Yields 4 servings

8 cups vegetable oil, for frying

1 Idaho potato

• Cut potatoes into 1/2-inch-by-1/2-inch-by-2-inch batons. In a fryer or deep, heavy-bottomed 4-quart pan, heat oil to 275°F. Blanch potato batons in oil until tender, about 10 minutes. Reserve frying oil.

*

black pepper–rubbed beef tenderloin

Yields 4 servings

1/2 tablespoon ground cumin

1/2 tablespoon kosher salt

2 tablespoons ground black pepper

1/2 tablespoon brown sugar

1 pound Kobe beef tenderloin, cut into four 1/4-pound portions (see Sources and Substitutions)

• In a sauté pan over medium heat, toss cumin for 1 minute to toast. Combine all ingredients except beef and mix thoroughly. Coat beef with mixture.

*

roasted red pepper puree

Yields 1/2 cup

1 red bell pepper

2 tablespoons vegetable oil

Kosher salt, to taste

2 cloves roasted garlic (see Basics, p. 267)

2 tablespoons extra-virgin olive oil

• Preheat oven to 350°F. Cut off top of pepper and remove seeds. Coat pepper with vegetable oil and sprinkle with salt. Place pepper on a rack on a baking pan and place in oven. Cook until pepper begins to brown and soften, about 30 minutes. Remove from oven and place in a bowl. Cover with plastic wrap to steam. Once cool, remove skin from pepper. Add the pepper to a blender with the roasted garlic and olive oil, and puree smooth.

putting it all together

• Heat oil reserved from papas al ajillo in a fryer or a deep, heavy-bottomed 4-quart pan to 375°F. Fry potato batons until golden brown, about 4 minutes. Remove from oil and drain.

• In a sauté pan over medium heat, heat garlic and parsley in olive oil until the mixture starts to sizzle. Add potato batons to pan and toss until coated. Season with salt.

• At the same time, heat a cast-iron skillet with 2 tablespoons vegetable oil over high heat. Sear beef on all sides except the ends. Beef should still be rare. Allow to rest 1 minute. Slice beef as thinly as possible and fan out on 4 plates. On the other side of each plate, stack the potato batons. Between the beef and potatoes place a roasted cipollini onion and a confit cherry tomato. Next to this, place a line of red pepper puree.

Madre y Hijo translates as "mother and son"—in this case, the chicken and the egg. This dish borrows from the Spanish tradition of topping meat or poultry with a fried egg. When the egg yolk is pierced, the liquid becomes a second sauce for the tender chicken.

serves 4

sous vide truffled chicken with fried eggs, rosemary fingerling potatoes, and truffled chicken jus

2 tablespoons chopped black truffle peels (see Sources and Substitutions)

2 tablespoons extra-virgin olive oil

3 tablespoons vegetable oil

* 4 servings sous vide chicken

Kosher salt, to taste

Black pepper, to taste

* 4 servings rosemary fingerling potatoes

5 tablespoons unsalted butter

4 large eggs

* 1 cup truffled chicken jus

*

sous vide chicken

Yields 4 servings

2 sprigs thyme

2 cups heavy cream

1/4 cup black truffle oil (see Sources and Substitutions)

3 cloves roasted garlic (see Basics, p. 267)

2 teaspoons kosher salt

2 (1/2-pound) skin-on boneless chicken breasts, cut in half

• Mix thyme, cream, truffle oil, roasted garlic, and salt together in a sealable bag. Add chicken and seal bag, removing as much air as possible. (A vacuum sealer works best.) Using a circulator or a saucepan filled with water over medium heat, bring the water to 155°F. Keep thermometer in the water and maintain a constant temperature. (For further explanation of this technique, see Basics, p. 278.) Place bag in water and cook 2 hours. Remove bag from water and shock in an ice bath.

*

rosemary fingerling potatoes

Yields 4 servings

6 fingerling potatoes, halved

1/4 cup rosemary leaves, finely chopped

Kosher salt, to taste

Extra-virgin olive oil, to coat

• Preheat oven to 500°F. Place a baking pan in the oven to heat, 5 minutes.

• In a bowl, toss all ingredients together until potatoes are well coated. Remove pan from oven and arrange potatoes cut side down. Reduce oven temperature to 375°F and cook potatoes until tender, about 18 minutes. Allow potatoes to cool to room temperature.

*

truffled chicken jus

Yields 1 cup

1/2 pound chicken bones

1/2 carrot, chopped

2 cups chopped Spanish onion

1/2 stalk celery, chopped

1 beefsteak tomato, chopped

1/4 cup tomato paste

12 cups chicken stock (see Basics, p. 268)

2 tablespoons black truffle oil (see Sources and Substitutions)

• Preheat oven to 500°F. Clean chicken bones of all fat and skin and place in a roasting pan. Place pan into oven and roast chicken bones until golden brown. Remove bones from the oven and place in a stockpot.

• Add carrots, onions, and celery to the roasting pan and place on the stovetop on high heat. Cook vegetables, stirring frequently, until all of the fond stuck to the bottom of the pan has come off. Add tomatoes and cook 15 minutes. Add tomato paste and cook 5 more minutes. Transfer everything to the stockpot with the chicken bones. Add stock. Heat mixture over high heat until it starts to boil. Reduce to a simmer. Cook for 2 hours, skimming all the fat off the top as it cooks, then strain mixture through a chinois. Return the liquid to the stockpot and cook over medium heat until reduced to 1 cup. Strain again. Whisk in truffle oil. Truffled chicken jus can be frozen for up to 2 weeks.

putting it all together

• Marinate truffle peels in extra-virgin olive oil for up to 1 hour. Preheat oven to 350°F. In a sauté pan over high heat, heat vegetable oil. Remove chicken from bag. Season with salt and pepper. Place chicken skin side down in hot pan. Once the skin is crisp and browned, flip chicken over and place in the oven to warm through, about 3 minutes.

• At the same time, in a separate sauté pan, combine fingerling potatoes with 2 tablespoons butter and place pan in the oven to heat, 3 minutes.

• In a sauté pan over low heat, heat 1 tablespoon butter and fry eggs sunny side up.

• In a saucepan over medium heat, heat truffled chicken jus. Once hot, add 2 tablespoons butter and whisk to emulsify.

• Remove the chicken and potatoes from the oven and divide potatoes among 4 plates. Place a piece of chicken on top of the potatoes. Spoon the truffled chicken jus over the chicken. With a ring mold about 3 inches in diameter cut out the eggs so you have mostly the yolks. Place a yolk on top of each piece of chicken. Garnish the plates with marinated truffle peels.

Sweetbreads are a French contribution to Basque cuisine. Here I've recreated a popular Basque recipe: The creamy sweetbreads are simply seared and paired with English peas and fava beans. (NOTE: The sweetbreads need to be soaked in milk a day in advance.)

serves 4

serrano ham-wrapped crispy sweetbreads with english peas and fava beans

1/2 cup fava beans

1/2 cup English peas

1 cup small-diced Spanish onion

4 tablespoons vegetable oil

* 1 1/4 cup chicken velouté

1 tablespoon unsalted butter

10 sprigs flat-leaf parsley, finely chopped

* 4 servings poached sweetbreads

4 slices serrano ham

2 ounces aged manchego cheese, shaved

✻

chicken velouté

Yields 1 1/4 cups

1/2 cup small-diced Spanish onion

1 clove garlic, minced

1 tablespoon vegetable oil

2 cups chicken stock (see Basics, p. 268)

1 teaspoon unsalted butter

1 teaspoon all-purpose flour

• In a saucepan over medium heat, lightly sauté onion and garlic in oil until soft. Add stock and reduce over high heat to 1 1/4 cups.

• In a separate saucepan over low heat, melt butter. Add flour slowly, stirring with a rubber spatula to prevent lumps. Cook this roux over low heat until a nutty aroma develops, about 5 minutes. Add reduced stock to roux and cook over low heat until sauce thickens, about 10 minutes. Velouté can be refrigerated for up to 2 days.

✻

poached sweetbreads

Yields 4 servings

1/2 pound sweetbreads

3 cups whole milk

1/2 carrot, chopped

2 cups chopped Spanish onion

1/2 stalk celery, chopped

2 bay leaves

2 cloves

2 tablespoons black peppercorns

1 cup white wine

1 cup water

1/3 cup kosher salt

• In a bowl, soak sweetbreads in milk with a light weight on top of them in the refrigerator overnight.

• In a saucepan, combine carrots, onions, celery, bay leaves, cloves, peppercorns, white wine, and water. Add salt and bring mixture to a boil over high heat. Reduce to a simmer.

• Peel any membrane off sweetbreads. Add sweetbreads to simmering liquid and poach 3 minutes. Drain sweetbreads, and again peel off as much of the membrane as possible. Divide sweetbreads into 4 pieces, and wrap in plastic.

putting it all together

• Preheat oven to 350°F. Bring a pot of water to a boil. Blanch fava beans for 2 minutes. Shock in an ice bath. Blanch English peas for 1 minute. Shock in an ice bath.

• In a sauté pan over low heat, sweat onions, English peas, and fava beans in 2 tablespoons vegetable oil until onions are translucent. Add chicken velouté and continue to cook over low heat for 1 minute. Remove from heat and stir in butter and chopped parsley.

• Remove sweetbreads from the plastic wrap and wrap in serrano ham slices. Heat remaining 2 tablespoons vegetable oil in a separate sauté pan over high heat and sear sweetbreads on all sides until browned. Place in oven to finish, 2 minutes.

• Pour the fava beans and peas into 4 shallow bowls, then place a portion of serrano ham-wrapped sweetbreads on top. Garnish with some manchego shavings.

A simple Peruvian dish—little more than chicken and rice, really—inspired me to make this marinated duck version. In Peru you'd find these elements combined, with the herbs cooked into the rice. But I discovered that you can get more flavor, color, and texture from the ingredients if you use each separately. (NOTE: You'll need to start marinating the duck two days in advance.)

serves 4

roasted duck breast and duck confit with green rice, sweet pea sauce, and tomatillo-jalapeño marmalade

* 4 servings marinated duck breasts

2 shallots, brunoised

3 cloves garlic, minced

2 tablespoons vegetable oil

1 cup shredded confit duck leg (see Basics, p. 276)

2 cups cooked white rice

1/4 cup finely chopped scallions

1/4 cup English peas

* 7 tablespoons verde puree

* 1/2 cup sweet pea sauce

* 2/3 cup tomatillo-jalapeño marmalade

3 tablespoons red chile oil (see Basics, p. 267)

*

marinated duck breasts

Yields 4 servings

1 1/2 teaspoons ground allspice

1/4 stick canela (see Sources and
Substitutions)

1 teaspoon juniper berries (see Sources and
Substitutions)

1 1/2 teaspoons ground star anise

1 navel orange, segmented

1/2 cup grenadine

2 tablespoons molasses

1/2 cup Triple Sec liqueur

1/4 cup soy sauce

1/2 cup brown sugar

1 tablespoon pink curing salt (see Sources
and Substitutions)

4 Peking duck breasts

• In a large sauté pan over high heat, toss
spices for 1 minute to toast. In a food
processor, combine all ingredients except
duck breasts, and puree. Strain through a
fine-mesh strainer.

• Score the skin of the duck with a knife.
Place duck in a plastic container with
marinade for 48 hours in the refrigerator.

*

verde puree

Yields 1/2 cup

1/4 cup cilantro leaves

1/4 cup flat-leaf parsley leaves

3/4 cup baby spinach

1 jalapeño chile, seeded and roughly
chopped

2 1/2 tablespoons chicken stock (see Basics,
p. 268)

2 1/2 tablespoons extra-virgin olive oil

2 1/2 tablespoons vegetable oil

1 clove garlic

Kosher salt, to taste

• Combine all ingredients in a blender and
puree until mixed but not completely
smooth. Puree can be refrigerated for up
to 2 days.

*

sweet pea sauce

Yields 1/2 cup

1/2 shallot, chopped

1 clove garlic, minced

1 tablespoon plus 1 teaspoon extra-virgin
olive oil

1/4 cup vegetable stock (see Basics, p. 270)

1/4 cup English peas

1 tablespoon chopped cilantro leaves

• In a saucepan over low heat, sweat
shallots and garlic in 1 teaspoon olive oil
until translucent. Add vegetable stock, and
bring to a boil. Reduce heat and simmer 5
minutes. Allow to cool. Transfer to a
blender and puree with peas, cilantro, and
remaining oil. Puree can be refrigerated
for up to 2 days.

*

tomatillo-jalapeño marmalade

Yields 2/3 cup

1/2 shallot, brunoised

1/2 minced teaspoon garlic

1/2 jalapeño chile, brunoised

1 tablespoon vegetable oil

2 tomatillos, diced small

1/2 tablespoon white wine vinegar

1/2 tablespoon corn syrup

1/2 tablespoon glucose syrup (see Sources and Substitutions)

1/2 tablespoon verde puree

• In a saucepan over low heat, sweat shallots, garlic, and jalapeño in vegetable oil until shallots are translucent. Add tomatillos, vinegar, corn syrup, and glucose syrup. Reduce over medium heat to a jam-like consistency. Add verde puree. Spread on a tray covered in plastic wrap to cool. Marmalade can be refrigerated for up to 1 week.

putting it all together

• Preheat oven to 350°F. In an ovenproof sauté pan over low heat, place duck breasts skin side down and cook until skin is dark brown. Flip duck breasts and place in oven until cooked to medium, about 6 minutes.

• In a sauté pan over medium heat, sweat shallots and garlic in vegetable oil until translucent. Add shredded duck confit, cooked rice, scallions, peas, and verde puree and warm over medium heat.

• Divide rice mixture among 4 plates. Slice each duck breast into 1/8-inch slices and arrange around the rice. Place sweet pea sauce next to the duck on one side and tomatillo-jalapeño marmalade on the other side. Drizzle plates with chile oil.

There are several steps to prepare the shredded confit pork in this recipe, but it's well worth it. The tender meat makes for an impressive dish and you won't need many sides to complete the meal. I serve a simple rosemary-brown butter applesauce, wilted escarole, and chicharrones—a Latin favorite. (NOTE: You'll need to brine the pork shanks and chicharrones overnight.)

serves 4

shredded confit pork with rosemary-brown butter applesauce and catalán escarole

1/2 cup all-purpose flour

* 4 servings shredded confit pork cubes

8 cups vegetable oil

* 1/4 cup rosemary-brown butter applesauce

* 1 1/2 cups Catalán escarole

1 tablespoon smoked paprika oil (see Basics, p. 268)

* 4 pieces chicharrones

*

shredded confit pork cubes

Yields 4 servings

2 cups granulated sugar

2 cups plus 1 teaspoon kosher salt

2 gallons water

2 (2-pound) pork shanks

Vegetable oil, to cover

6 sheets gelatin

2 cups chicken stock (See Basics, p. 268)

1 tablespoon chopped thyme leaves

1 teaspoon chopped rosemary leaves

• Combine sugar, 2 cups kosher salt, and water in a container large enough to fit pork shanks. Add pork and brine overnight in the refriferator.

• Preheat oven to 250°F. Remove pork from brine; discard brine. Using a filet knife, cut the bones from the shanks. Place meat in a deep pan and cover with oil. Cover pan tightly with two layers of aluminum foil. Place in the oven to cook, 3 hours and 15 minutes. Remove the shanks from the oven and take them out of the oil. Discard the oil.

• Increase oven temperature to 300°F. Place shanks on a roasting rack on a sheet tray. Cook 20 minutes. Remove shanks from oven and shred meat into a bowl.

• Bloom gelatin in ice water. Squeeze out excess water. In a saucepan over low heat, heat chicken stock and season with 1 teaspoon salt. Add gelatin to dissolve. Add stock and herbs to shredded meat. Mix well. Press into a 3-inch-by-12-inch-by-3-inch mold. Place a weight on top of the meat and refrigerate to set, 8 hours. Unmold meat and cut into four 2-inch cubes, discarding the edges.

*

rosemary—brown butter

applesauce

Yields 3/4 cup

3 Granny Smith apples, peeled and chopped

2 tablespoons granulated sugar

1/4 cup plus 1/2 tablespoon unsalted butter

2 tablespoons apple cider

2 tablespoons rosemary leaves

• In a saucepan over low heat, sweat apples with sugar and 1/2 tablespoon butter until soft.

• In a separate saucepan over medium heat, melt 1/4 cup butter and cook until it browns. Add browned butter, apple cider, and rosemary to apple mixture. Bring to a simmer over medium heat and cook until apples are very tender. Pour the mixture into a food processor and puree until smooth. Chill. Rosemary—brown butter applesauce can be refrigerated for up to 2 days.

*

catalán escarole

Yields 1 1/2 cups

1 cup pine nuts

3 tablespoons unsalted butter

Kosher salt, to taste

3 shallots, brunoised

3 cloves garlic, minced

2 tablespoons vegetable oil

1 cup dried black currants

1 head escarole, cut into a chiffonade

1 guindilla chile, cut into a chiffonade (see
  Sources and Substitutions)

• In a sauté pan over medium heat, toss
pine nuts to toast. Add 1 tablespoon
butter and a sprinkle of salt. Continue to
toss until butter has melted and coated
the nuts.

• In a saucepan over low heat, sweat
shallots and garlic in vegetable oil until
translucent. Add pine nuts and currants
and cook over low heat 1 minute. Turn the
heat up to high and add escarole and
guindillas and season with salt. Stir
escarole until it starts to wilt. Add 2
tablespoons butter and toss until melted.
Use immediately.

*

chicharrones

Yields 4 pieces

16 cups water

1/2 cup kosher salt

1/2 cup granulated sugar

1/2 pound pork skin

• In a bowl, combine water, salt, and sugar.
Stir until sugar is dissolved. Place pork skin
in the mixture and refrigerate overnight.
Remove the skin from the mixture and
place in a pan on a roasting rack. Let pork
skin dry at room temperature for 1 hour.
Preheat oven to 225°F. Bake pork skin for 6
hours. Cut into 4 equal pieces.

putting it all together

• Preheat oven to 350°F. Dredge shredded
confit pork cubes in flour. In a fryer or
deep, heavy-bottomed 4-quart pan, heat
vegetable oil to 340°F. Fry cubes until
golden brown. Drain cubes, then bake 5
minutes until heated.

• In a saucepan over medium heat, heat
rosemary–brown butter applesauce.

• On each of 4 plates, place a pile of the
escarole in one corner. Using 1 tablespoon
rosemary–brown butter applesauce, streak
a line in the opposite corner. Place a
shredded confit pork cube in another
corner and top with a chicharrone. Drizzle
paprika oil in the remaining corner.

This recipe takes its influences from all over Mexico—for instance, the marinated chicken borrows its achiote, orange, and garlic flavors from Yucatán cooking—and from Zarella Martinez, whose cookbooks inspired me to experiment with chile-spiced cornbread.

serves 4

roasted chicken breast with poblano cornbread, charred pineapple, and red chile sauce

* 4 servings poblano cornbread
* 1 cup red chile sauce

  3 tablespoons vegetable oil
* 4 servings marinated chicken breasts

  Kosher salt, to taste

  Black pepper, to taste
* 1/2 cup charred pineapple

＊

poblano cornbread

Yields 6 servings

Nonstick cooking spray

1 cup unsalted butter

1/2 pound granulated sugar

4 large eggs

2 cups rice flour

1 tablespoon baking powder

1 teaspoon kosher salt

6 ounces white cheddar cheese, grated
(about 3 cups)

1 1/2 cups roasted poblano chiles, diced
small (see Basics, p. 273)

2 cups corn kernels (from about 3 ears)

• Preheat oven to 300°F. Generously grease
a 9-inch-square baking pan with nonstick
cooking spray. In a mixer, combine butter
and sugar. Whip on high speed with paddle
attachment until creamy. Add eggs one at
a time, mixing well between additions.

• In a separate bowl, combine flour, baking
powder, salt, and cheese, and mix well. Add
dry ingredients to mixer and combine. Fold
in chiles and corn by hand. Pour batter into
baking pan and tap the pan to level. Bake
until a toothpick comes out clean, about 45
minutes. Allow to cool before removing
from pan. Once cooled, remove from pan
and cut into 6 pieces. Cornbread can be
refrigerated, wrapped in plastic wrap, for
up to 1 day.

＊

red chile sauce

Yields 1 cup

1/2 large Spanish onion

1/4 cup guajillo chile paste (see Basics, p. 271)

2 roasted plum tomatoes (see Basics, p. 273)

3 cloves roasted garlic (see Basics, p. 267)

2 tablespoons cup lard

1/2 cup chicken stock (see Basics, p. 268)

• Place onion on a grill or open-flame
burner to char, and then roughly chop.

• In a blender, combine onions, guajillo chile
paste, roasted tomatoes, and roasted
garlic. Puree until smooth.

• In a saucepan over high heat, melt lard.
Add puree and fry until aromatic, 5 to 7
minutes. Add chicken stock and bring
mixture to a boil. Remove from heat, strain
through a fine-mesh strainer, and chill.
Sauce can be refrigerated for up to 2
days.

✷

marinated chicken breasts

Yields 4 servings

1/4 cup achiote (see Sources and
   Substitutions)

8 cloves garlic

2 navel oranges, juiced

1 cup grapeseed oil

5 teaspoons cilantro leaves

2 guajillo chiles, seeded (see Sources and
   Substitutions)

4 (6-ounce) skin-on chicken breasts

• Combine all ingredients except chicken
breasts in a blender and puree until
smooth. Place chicken breasts in a
container and pour marinade over the
chicken. Marinate for at least 4 hours.

✷

charred pineapple

Yields 1/2 cup

Nonstick cooking spray

4 (1/2-inch-thick) slices pineapple

1/4 cup extra-virgin olive oil

1 tablespoon cilantro chiffonade

1 shallot, brunoised

• Coat grill with nonstick cooking spray.
Over a high flame, grill pineapple slices
until grill marks form, about 1 minute per
side. Remove from the grill and chill. Once
cool cut pineapple into medium dice. In a
bowl, toss pineapple with remaining
ingredients.

putting it all together

• Preheat oven to 400°F. Place cornbread
on a baking sheet in oven to warm and
brown, about 3 minutes.

• In a saucepan over medium heat, heat red
chile sauce.

• In an ovenproof sauté pan over high heat,
heat vegetable oil. Season chicken with salt
and pepper and then place the chicken skin
side down in the pan. Once golden brown,
flip over and place in the oven until cooked
through, about 5 minutes.

• Draw a large circle of red chile sauce on
each of 4 plates. Place cornbread in the
middle of the sauce, and then place the
chicken breast on top of cornbread.
Arrange charred pineapple in a line next to
the chicken.

There are some things that just can't be improved upon—like this classic, complex Mexican mole made with Ibarra chocolate. But other aspects are easily updated. In my recipe, instead of simmering the turkey meat in the mole, I cook it sous vide before adding it to the sauce. The result is an equally flavorful dish, with a better texture.

serves 4

turkey mole
with refried beans
and ibarra chocolate shavings

* 2 cups mole sauce

* 2 cups refried beans

  3 tablespoons vegetable oil

* 4 servings sous vide turkey breast

  1/8 disk Ibarra chocolate, zested (see Sources and Substitutions)

  2 tablespoons black sesame seeds

*

mole sauce

Yields 2 cups

1/4 cup pepitas (see Sources and Substitutions)

1/4 cup almonds

1/4 cup sesame seeds

1 plum tomato

4 cups vegetable oil, for frying

1/2 guajillo chile, seeded (see Sources and Substitutions)

1/2 ancho chile, seeded (see Sources and Substitutions)

1/2 mulatto chile, seeded (see Sources and Substitutions)

1 pasilla chile, seeded (see Sources and Substitutions)

1 Granny Smith apple, chopped

1 sweet plantain, chopped

1/4 pound lard

4 cups chopped Spanish onion

5 cloves roasted garlic (see Basics, see p. 267)

2 tablespoons raisins

3 cups chicken stock (see Basics, p. 268)

1/4 cup crushed tortilla chips

1/8 disk Ibarra chocolate (see Sources and Substitutions)

• In a sauté pan over high heat, toss nuts and seeds for 1 minute to toast.

• Char tomato over an open flame until blackened on all sides. Chop tomato.

• In a fryer or a deep, heavy-bottomed 2-quart pan, heat vegetable oil to 375°F. Blanch chiles in oil for 5 seconds, then place in a container of water to cool.

• Blanch apples and plantains in oil until dark brown but not burnt.

• In a saucepan over low heat, melt 2 ounces lard; sweat onions and roasted garlic in lard until onions are translucent. Add toasted pepitas, almonds, and sesame seeds, and cook for 15 minutes to extract oils. Add tomatoes, apples, plantains, and raisins, and cook over low heat until you get a sauce-like consistency, about 1 hour. Add toasted chiles, stock, and tortilla chips. Bring mixture to a boil, then reduce to a simmer and cook for 1 hour. In a food processor, puree sauce, and pass mixture through a fine china cap.

• In another saucepan over high heat, melt the remaining 2 ounces lard and heat until smoking. Add mole to refry and reduce heat to a very low simmer. Stir in chocolate, and cook uncovered for 2 hours. Mole can be refrigerated for up to 2 days.

*

sous vide turkey breast

Yields 4 servings

1 pound turkey breast

3/4 cup duck fat

4 cloves garlic

4 sprigs thyme

2 teaspoons kosher salt

• Pack all ingredient into a sealable plastic bag and remove as much air as possible. (A vacuum sealer works best.) Using a circulator or a pan filled with water over medium heat, bring the water to 155°F. Keep a thermometer in the water and maintain a constant temperature. (For further explanation of this technique, see Basics, p. 278.) Place bag in water and cook for 2 hours. Remove bag from water and shock in an ice bath. Remove the turkey from bag and cut into large dice.

---

putting it all together

• In separate saucepans over low heat, heat mole sauce and refried beans.

• In a sauté pan over high heat, heat vegetable oil. Sear turkey cubes in hot oil on all sides.

• Smear a line of hot mole on each of 4 plates. Place 3 turkey cubes in the line of mole and top with chocolate zest. Next to the mole smear a line of refried beans. Place 3 turkey cubes in the line of beans and sprinkle with sesame seeds.

*

refried beans

Yields 2 cups

1 cup chopped Spanish onion

1 clove garlic, sliced

1/2 chipotle chile, sliced

2 tablespoons lard

2/3 pound dried pinto beans, soaked in water overnight

1 bay leaf

1 tablespoon Mexican oregano leaves (see Sources and Substitutions)

3 cups water

Kosher salt, to taste

• In a saucepan over low heat, sweat onions, garlic, and chipotles in 1 tablespoon lard until onions are translucent. Add beans, bay leaf, oregano, and water and cook until soft, about 1 1/2 hours. Puree mixture in a blender.

• In a separate saucepan over high heat, melt remaining 1 tablespoon lard until smoking. Pour in the bean puree and refry. Reduce heat to low and cook 30 minutes. Season with salt. Refried beans can be refrigerated for up to 2 days.

You can find vaca frita—which translates to "fried cow"—everywhere in Cuba. There it's served simply, with white rice, black beans, and avocado. I've found different ways to present those familiar flavors, adding new textures to the traditional recipe. (NOTE: You'll need to soak the beans a day in advance.)

serves 4

vaca frita
with black bean broth
and creamy rice croquettes

1 avocado

2 tablespoons lemon juice

* 2 cups black bean broth

8 cups vegetable oil, for frying, plus 1/4 cup

* 4 servings vaca frita

1/4 cup finely chopped scallions

1 1/4 cups shaved red onion

* 8 creamy rice croquettes

1 large beefsteak tomato

4 teaspoons cilantro pods

*

black bean broth

Yields 2 cups

1/4 pound dried black beans, picked and
    soaked overnight in water

2 cups water

1 bay leaf

1/4 teaspoon white vinegar

1/2 teaspoon kosher salt

3 cloves roasted garlic (see Basics, p. 267)

1/4 cup onion confit (see Basics, p. 272)

1/4 roasted green bell pepper (see Basics,
    p. 273)

4 1/2 tablespoons extra-virgin olive oil

1/2 teaspoon dried oregano

• Rinse beans. In a saucepan over high heat,
combine beans, water, bay leaf, vinegar, and
salt. Bring mixture to a boil. Reduce heat
and simmer until beans are slightly tender,
about 1 hour.

• In a blender, combine garlic, onion confit,
and bell pepper. Puree until smooth. In a
saucepan over high heat, heat olive oil. Add
vegetable puree then turn down heat to
medium. Add beans and oregano and
simmer 30 minutes. Once the beans are
fully cooked, puree with a hand blender.
Broth should remain slightly chunky. Broth
can be refrigerated for 2 to 3 days.

*

vaca frita

Yields 4 servings

1/4 cup black peppercorns

1/2 cup mustard seeds

3/4 cup pickling spice

1/4 cup red pepper flakes

16 cups water

16 cloves garlic

1/4 cup kosher salt

2 1/2 pounds skirt steak, trimmed

• Preheat oven to 300°F. In a roasting pan
over high heat, combine peppercorns,
mustard seeds, pickling spice, and red
pepper flakes, and toast over medium heat
until aromatic, stirring frequently. Add
water, garlic, and salt to roasting pan. Add
meat, turning to ensuring that the spice
mixture is evenly distributed. Add
additional water to cover beef, if
necessary. Bring liquid to a boil and then
cover pan with aluminum foil and place in
oven. Cook for 2 hours.

• Remove pan from oven and allow meat to
cool in liquid to room temperature.
Transfer meat to parchment-lined plate
and refrigerate until completely cooled.
Once cooled, cut into 4 equal pieces, wrap
in plastic wrap, and refrigerate.

*

creamy rice croquettes

Yields 8 croquettes

1 sheet gelatin

3/4 cup béchamel (see Basics, p. 274)

3 ounces queso fresco, diced small
(about 1/4 cup)

1/2 cup cooked long grain rice

1 tablespoon chopped thyme leaves

1 tablespoon flat-leaf parsley chiffonade

Kosher salt, to taste

Black pepper, to taste

1 cup all-purpose flour

5 large eggs, whisked

1 cup finely ground bread crumbs

• Bloom gelatin in ice water. Squeeze out
excess liquid.

• In a saucepan over low heat, heat béchamel,
then stir in gelatin until dissolved. In a
bowl, combine béchamel, cheese, rice, thyme,
parsley, salt, and pepper, and fold together
until thoroughly mixed. Place a piece of
parchment on a tray then pour mixture
onto tray. Place in refrigerator to cool.
Once cooled, roll mixture into 8 oval balls.

• To bread croquettes, arrange 3 large bowls
in a line. Place flour in the first, whisked eggs
in the second, and bread crumbs in third.
Drop croquettes into flour, shaking bowl until
croquettes are completely coated. Remove
croquettes from flour, shaking off excess, and
put into bowl with eggs. Shake bowl until
croquettes are completely covered in egg.
Remove croquettes from egg, shake off
excess, and put into bowl with bread crumbs.
Shake bowl until croquettes are evenly
coated. Remove croquettes from bread
crumbs, shake off excess, and place on a tray
lined with parchment paper. Croquettes can
be refrigerated, uncovered, for up to 3 days.

putting it all together

• Cut balls out of the avocado to make
pearls. (A small Persian cutter works well.)
Drop the pearls into water with 1/2
teaspoon lemon juice to retain color.

• In a saucepan over low heat, heat the
black bean broth.

• In a large cast-iron skillet over high heat,
heat 1/4 cup vegetable oil until almost
smoking. Place vaca frita in the pan and
sear, about 1 minute. Flip vaca frita over
and add scallions, red onion, and remaining
lemon juice. Cook 1 minute.

• In a fryer or deep heavy-bottomed
4-quart pan, heat 8 cups vegetable oil to
375°F and fry croquettes until golden
brown, about 3 minutes.

• To prepare beefsteak tomato, cut off
the top and bottom of the tomato. Remove
the outside skin, leaving the four hearts
exposed. With paring knife, carefully
remove each heart from the core.

• Divide black bean broth among 4 shallow
bowls. Place vaca frita in each bowl and
top with red onions and scallions. Garnish
the bowls with tomato hearts, avocado
pearls, and rice croquettes. Sprinkle with
cilantro pods.

Braised lamb shank served with crisp potato chips is a casual Basque dish. To transform it into dinner-party fare, I've replaced the shank with an attractive rack of lamb, and the rich braise is lightened with artichoke and lemon.

serves 4

roasted rack of lamb with papas fritas, marinated artichokes, artichoke puree, and candied lemons

1 tablespoon vegetable oil

* 4 servings marinated lamb

Kosher salt, to taste

Black pepper, to taste

3 tablespoons unsalted butter, melted

* 1/4 cup artichoke puree

* 1/2 cup sherry lamb jus

* 4 pieces candied lemon peel

* 1 cup marinated artichokes

* 4 servings papas fritas

✳

marinated lamb

Yields 4 servings

2 racks New Zealand lamb, cut in half

10 cloves garlic, minced

1/2 cup plus 2 tablespoons thyme leaves, chopped fine

1 1/8 cup rosemary leaves, chopped fine

1 cup extra-virgin olive oil

• Place lamb racks in a container and cover with garlic, herbs, and oil. Marinate for 6 hours.

✳

artichoke puree

Yields 1/3 cup

1 confit artichoke, stem removed (see Basics, p. 271)

3 tablespoons vegetable stock (see Basics, p. 270)

1 clove roasted garlic (see Basics, p. 267)

2 tablespoons lemon juice

1/2 teaspoon kosher salt

1/8 teaspoon black pepper

• In a blender, combine all ingredients and puree until smooth. Pass through a tamis. Puree can be refrigerated for up to 2 days.

✳

sherry lamb jus

Yields 2 cups

2 1/2 pounds lamb bones

8 cups chopped Spanish onions

1 1/2 carrots, chopped

2 stalks celery, chopped

3 beefsteak tomatoes, chopped

7 sprigs thyme

1/2 tablespoon black peppercorns

1/2 cup tomato paste

2 gallons water

2 cups sherry

• Preheat oven to 500°F. Place bones in a roasting pan and roast until bones have browned, about 30 minutes. Pull the pan out twice during roasting to drain off the fat. Put bones into a pot and set aside.

• Add onions, carrots, and celery to the roasting pan and place on top of the stove over high heat. Cook until the bottom of the pan is cleaned, stirring frequently. Add tomatoes, thyme, and peppercorns and cook 15 minutes. Then add tomato paste and cook 5 more minutes.

• Add vegetables to the pot with the bones and pour in the water. Place on the stove and bring to a boil over high heat. Reduce heat and bring to a simmer. Skim the fat throughout the entire cooking process. Simmer the stock for 5 hours then strain out solids and return all the liquid to the pot. Reduce on high heat to 2 cups.

• In a separate pot reduce sherry over high heat to a syrup then add to the lamb jus. Place in the refrigerator to cool. Sherry lamb jus can be frozen for up to 1 month.

*

candied lemon peels

Yields about 16 pieces

6 cups water

Peel of 1 lemon, all white pith removed,
    sliced into 16 thin strips

2 cups granulated sugar, plus sugar for
    sprinkling

• In a saucepan, bring 2 cups water to a
boil. Blanch lemon peels for 1 minute and
shock in ice water. Discard blanching water
and repeat process with 2 more cups
water. Then bring to 2 cups water and
sugar to a boil. Blanch lemon peels a third
time for 1 minute and shock in ice water.
Remove peels and place on a nonstick
surface, such as a Silpat, and sprinkle with
sugar. Candied lemons can be stored at
room temperature in a dry area for up to
1 week.

*

marinated artichokes

Yields 1 cup

2 confit artichokes, sliced thin (see Basics,
    p. 271)

1 tablespoon chopped black truffle peels
    (see Sources and Substitutions)

2 tablespoons lemon juice

2 tablespoons extra-virgin olive oil

2 tablespoons black truffle oil (see Sources
    and Substitutions)

1/2 teaspoon kosher salt

5 sprigs flat-leaf parsley, finely chopped

• In a bowl, combine all ingredients and mix
well. Refrigerate, at least 2 hours.
Marinated artichokes can be refrigerated,
in oil, for up to 1 month.

*

papas fritas

Yields 4 servings

8 cups vegetable oil, for frying

1 Idaho potato, peeled and sliced paper
    thin

Kosher salt, to taste

• In a fryer or deep, heavy-bottomed 4-
quart pan, heat vegetable oil to 265°F.
Working in small batches, drop sliced
potatoes into the fryer and fry until
slightly browned and crisp, about 5
minutes. Remove from the fryer and drain.
Season with salt.

putting it all together

• Preheat oven to 400°F. In a cast-iron
skillet over medium heat, heat vegetable
oil. Season lamb racks with salt and pepper.
Place lamb in the hot pan and place in the
oven to roast, 4 to 5 minutes. Turn lamb
over and cook another 4 or 5 minutes.
Lamb is best at medium-rare to medium;
try not to overcook it. Baste lamb with
butter and allow it to rest for 1 minute.

• In a small saucepan over low heat, heat
artichoke puree.

• Using the artichoke puree, make a streak
on each plate. Cut the lamb meat off the
bone, then slice it into pieces. Place the
bones on the plate next to the puree then
layer the meat over the bones. Drizzle each
plate with 2 tablespoons lamb jus. Garnish
with candied lemon peels and marinated
artichokes. Serve with papas fritas.

postres

desserts

Everywhere I went in the Basque region, I saw this French almond cake. There are many different recipes for it; I was inspired by those filled with pastry cream and cherries. Amarena Fabbri black cherries are grown and packaged in Italy, not Spain, but I can't resist their decadent flavor.

serves 4

gâteaux basques
with pastry cream, cherry cream,
and cherry sauce

* 1/4 cup cherry sauce

* 4 Basque cakes

* 1/4 cup pastry cream

* 1 cup cherry cream

Cake crumbs reserved from Basque cakes

4 blanched almonds, crushed

4 sweet Amarena Fabbri cherries (see Sources and Substitutions)

★

cherry sauce and cherry cream

Yields 3/4 cup sauce and 1 1/4 cups cream

1 cup sweet Amarena Fabbri cherries (see
    Sources and Substitutions)

1/2 cup heavy cream

• In a food processor, puree cherries until
smooth. Reserve 3/4 cup of puree to use as
a sauce. Whip cream until soft peaks form.
Slowly add 1/4 cup cherry puree to cream,
and whip until stiff peaks form.

★

basque cakes

Yields four 4-inch cakes, plus cake crumbs

1 cup unsalted butter, softened, plus more
    for greasing pans

3/4 cup granulated sugar

1 teaspoon kosher salt

1 large egg

1 large egg yolk

2 lemons, zested

1 tablespoon almond flour (see Sources and
    Substitutions)

1 1/3 cups all-purpose flour

• Preheat oven to 325°F. By hand, whisk butter
and sugar in a bowl. Add salt, whole egg, and
yolk; whisk well. Add lemon zest and almond
flour; whisk until smooth. Using a spatula,
fold in all-purpose flour until just incorporated.
Let rest while preparing pans.

• Generously brush the sides of four 4-inch
tart rings with butter. Spread the batter
evenly into rings. Do not fill more than 3/4 full.
Place rings on a baking sheet. Bake until just
browned around the edges, 25 to 30 minutes.
Remove cakes from the oven and immediately
scoop out a shallow hole 1 inch in diameter
from the center of each cake. Save scraps.

• Crumble cake scraps on a sheet tray and
bake for 15 to 20 minutes at 325°F until
just browned. Allow to cool, then store in
an airtight container.

• Allow cakes to cool in the rings. When
cooled, remove from rings, and store in an
airtight container until ready to use. Cakes
are best used the same day they are
made, but they can be frozen up to 5 days.

★

pastry cream

Yields 2 cups

3 tablespoons cornstarch

3/4 cup granulated sugar

6 large egg yolks

1 cup whole milk

1/2 vanilla bean, scraped

• In a bowl, whisk together cornstarch and
sugar. Add egg yolks and mix until smooth. In a
saucepan over high heat, heat milk and vanilla
seeds and bean until boiling. Add half of the
hot milk mixture to the egg yolk mixture,
whisking. Then return egg yolk–milk mixture
to the saucepan and whisk into remaining
milk. Return saucepan to high heat, and whisk
until mixture boils and thickens. Remove
vanilla bean and pour pastry cream into a
bowl. Cover the bowl with plastic resting on
the pastry cream. Chill until needed. Pastry
cream can be stored for up to 2 days.

putting it all together

• Brush 1 tablespoon cherry sauce on each
of 4 plates. Place a Basque cake slightly
off-center on each. Fill each cake with 1
tablespoon pastry cream and top with 1/4
cup cherry cream. Sprinkle with cake crumbs
and crushed almonds. Top each with a cherry.

Most of my desserts are collaborations between restaurant staff members and different Latin traditions. The results are creative desserts like this one, with a hodgepodge of influences. I love the balance between the creamy, mild avocado and crisp, acidic pineapple.

serves 4

avocado mousse with fresh pineapple, green tea meringues, and meyer lemon ice cream

* 16 strips candied pineapple
* 16 rounds avocado mousse
* 1/2 cup Pedro Ximénez reduction
* 16 fresh pineapple squares

  1/4 cup turbinado sugar
* 16 green tea meringues
* 1/2 cup Meyer lemon ice cream

*

candied pineapple and fresh

pineapple squares

Yields 16 candied strips and 16 squares

1 large pineapple

1 cup simple syrup (see Basics, p. 278)

• Begin by cutting off top and bottom of pineapple. Working from top to bottom cut away rind so that only fruit remains. Cut off fruit on opposite sides of the tough core. Cut off the smaller pieces on remaining sides of the core. Discard the core and the rinds. Take the 2 smaller pieces and square off into 2 even rectangles, roughly 1/2 inch by 4 inches. Slice 4-inch strips of pineapple from these rectangles as thinly as possible. The yield should be at least 16 strips. Place the strips in simple syrup, wrap in plastic and microwave for 3 minutes. Remove pineapple from syrup and lay out to cool. With remaining larger pieces of pineapple, cut 1/4-inch-thick strips. Cut the strips into 1-inch squares. The yield should be at least 16 pieces.

*

avocado mousse

Yields about 18 rounds

2 sheets gelatin

3/4 cup granulated sugar

3/4 cup water

2 avocados

2 tablespoons lemon juice

1 cup heavy cream

• Line an 8-inch square cake pan with plastic. In a bowl of ice water, bloom gelatin sheets. Squeeze out excess water.

• In a saucepan over high heat, combine sugar and water; heat until boiling. Remove from heat, and add bloomed gelatin. Stir until dissolved. Cool to room temperature.

• In a food processor, combine avocado pulp and lemon juice, and process until smooth and creamy. Slowly pour cooled syrup into avocado mixture, and process until smooth. Pour mixture into a bowl.

• In the bowl of an electric mixer, whip cream until soft peaks form. Do not overwhip. Fold whipped cream into avocado mixture until uniform. Pour mousse into prepared cake pan. Place in freezer until completely frozen, about 4 hours. Using a 3/4-inch round cutter, cut out rounds of avocado mousse. Place rounds on a tray, cover, and freeze again. Discard excess scraps.

*

pedro ximénez reduction

Yields 1 1/4 cups

1 cup Pedro Ximénez vinegar (see Sources and Substitutions)

1 cup glucose syrup (see Sources and Substitutions)

• In a saucepan over high heat, reduce vinegar to 1/4 cup. Add glucose syrup and stir until uniform. Allow to cool.

*

green tea meringues

Yields twenty five to thirty 1/2-inch
    meringues

3/4 cup granulated sugar

6 tablespoons water

4 bags green tea

1 large egg white

• Preheat oven to 225°F. In a saucepan over high heat, combine sugar and water. Heat to boiling. Remove from heat and add 3 tea bags. Steep for 3 minutes. Remove tea bags, return syrup to stove, and heat to 238°F.

• While syrup is boiling, begin to whip egg whites to soft peaks with a hand mixer. When syrup reaches temperature, slowly pour it into egg whites while whipping. Whip until cool. Using a pastry bag, pipe dime-size disks of meringue onto a nonstick, ovenproof surface, such as a Silpat. Cut open remaining tea bag and grind leaves into a powder using a spice grinder. Sprinkle ground tea over disks. Place trays in the oven and allow to dry out, 45 to 60 minutes. Meringues are done when they dissolve in the mouth and are no longer chewy. Meringues can be stored in airtight containers for up to 1 week.

*

meyer lemon ice cream

Yields 4 cups

1 1/2 Meyer lemons

6 tablespoons granulated sugar

1 tablespoon glucose syrup (see Sources
    and Substitutions)

1 cup heavy cream

1/2 cup whole milk

• Zest and juice lemons. Juice should yield 2 3/4 tablespoons. In a saucepan over high heat, heat sugar, glucose syrup, lemon juice, and zest until sugar has dissolved. Add cream and milk. Cool mixture completely. Churn in an ice cream machine according to manufacturer's instructions. The ice cream can be made up to 3 days ahead, but it's best served the day it is churned.

putting it all together

• Take cooled strips of pineapple and wrap around frozen avocado mousse rounds. Allow wrapped mousse to sit at room temperature for at least 10 minutes to defrost. Drizzle 2 tablespoons Pedro Ximénez reduction on each of 4 chilled plates. Randomly place 4 wrapped mousse rounds in the sauce.

• Line a sheet tray with aluminum foil. Stand pineapple cubes upright and sprinkle with turbinado sugar. Place under broiler for 30 seconds to melt and caramelize the sugar. A small torch could also be used to brûlée the sugar on the pineapple.

• Place the pineapple squares next to the avocado mousse. Place a green tea meringue next to each piece of pineapple. Scoop Meyer lemon ice cream in the center of the mousses. Serve immediately.

This is the Spanish answer to crème brûlée—a must-have dessert in any American restaurant. In the Catalán region of Spain, the custardy dessert is flavored with citrus and cinnamon, but our version holds a surprise: a frozen center of strawberry gelée to contrast with the custard.

serves 4

cremas catalanas with strawberry gelée, sangría reduction, almond-cocoa nib praline, canela tuiles, and grand marnier whipped cream

6 blackberries

* 4 cremas Catalanas

* 4 teaspoons almond-cocoa nib praline

* 1/4 cup sangría reduction

* 1/2 cup Grand Marnier whipped cream

* 8 canela tuiles

1/2 cup turbinado sugar

*

cremas catalanas

Yields 4 cremas Catalanas

1/2 sheet gelatin

1/2 teaspoon powdered agar (see Sources and Substitutions)

1/4 cup whole milk

3/4 cup plus 2 tablespoons heavy cream

1/4 cup granulated sugar

1/2 tablespoon dried lavender (see Sources and Substitutions)

3 large egg yolks

4 pieces strawberry gelée (see following recipe)

• In a bowl of ice water, bloom gelatin. Squeeze out excess water. In a saucepan over high heat, combine agar and milk and bring to a boil. Remove from heat and allow to cool.

• In a saucepan over high heat, heat cream with sugar and lavender until boiling. Remove from heat. In a separate bowl, whisk yolks. Pour cream mixture into yolks, whisking, to temper. Rinse out pot and then strain tempered mixture back into pot. Whisk in milk mixture. Return to high heat and bring to 185°F, stirring constantly. Add bloomed gelatin and stir until dissolved.

• Pour crema Catalana to almost fill four 1/2-cup oval silicone molds. Allow to rest until almost set. Before crema Catalana has set completely, place a strip of frozen strawberry gelée inside, making sure to push the gelée deep enough that the crema Catalana covers it completely. Freeze until completely frozen, about 8 hours. Remove crema Catalana from molds. Place on serving plates and refrigerate for 2 hours until thawed.

strawberry gelée

Yields 64 pieces

1/2 sheet gelatin

1 cup strawberries

6 tablespoons granulated sugar

1/4 cup water

• Line an 8-inch-by-4-inch loaf pan with plastic. In a bowl of ice water, bloom gelatin. Squeeze out excess water. In a saucepan over high heat, combine strawberries, sugar, and water. Cook until sugar has dissolved and strawberries have started to break down, 5 to 6 minutes. In a food processor, puree until smooth. Add bloomed gelatin and mix until smooth. Pour into prepared pan and place in freezer until completely frozen, about 4 hours. Remove from pan and cut into 2-inch-by-1/4-inch strips. Freeze again. Strawberry gelée can be frozen for up to 1 week.

*

almond–cocoa nib praline

Yields 1 1/4 cups

1/4 cup granulated sugar

1 tablespoon water

3/4 cup almonds

1/2 teaspoon baking powder

1/2 tablespoon kosher salt

1/4 cup cocoa nibs

• Preheat oven to 325°F. In a saucepan over high heat, heat sugar and water until caramelized.

• Place almonds on a sheet tray and bake until toasted, 6 to 7 minutes. While still warm, add almonds to caramel.

• Add baking powder, and stir until evenly dispersed. Baking powder will cause the caramel to spit, so be cautious. Spread evenly on a nonstick surface, such as a Silpat. Cool. In a food processor, grind to a coarse crumb. Add salt and cocoa nibs and mix until evenly dispersed. Store in an airtight container.

*

sangría reduction

Yields 6 tablespoons

1 cup red sangria

1 tablespoon granulated sugar

2 tablespoons glucose syrup (see Sources and Substitutions)

• In a saucepan over high heat, reduce sangría with sugar to 1/4 cup. Stir in glucose syrup, and cool.

*

grand marnier whipped cream

Yields 1 cup

1/2 cup heavy cream

5 tablespoons confectioners' sugar, or more to taste

2 tablespoons Grand Marnier

• In the bowl of an electric mixer, combine ingredients and whip to stiff peaks. Refrigerate until needed.

*

canela tuiles

Yields 8 tuiles

1 cup granulated sugar

1 cup water

1 sheet phyllo dough

2 tablespoons ground canela (see Sources and Substitutions)

• Preheat oven to 325°F. In a saucepan over high heat, boil sugar and water for 2 minutes to make simple syrup. Cool. Working quickly, generously brush phyllo dough with simple syrup. Sprinkle canela evenly over sheet. Cut into 8 equal pieces. Tightly wrap each piece of soaked phyllo dough around a skewer. Remove from skewer and place on a baking sheet lined with parchment. Bake until crisp, 15 to 20 minutes.

putting it all together

• Halve 2 of the fresh blackberries. Remove plates with cremas Catalanas from the refrigerator. Spoon a thin, curved line of almond–cocoa nib praline to the left of each crema Catalana. On the right, drizzle a line of sangría reduction and top with a halved and a full blackberry. Scoop Grand Marnier cream to the right of the blackberries and top with 2 canela tuiles. Sprinkle cremas Catalanas with turbinado sugar and caramelize the sugar using a small brûlée torch. (If you don't have a blowtorch, preheat broiler. Place cremas Catalanas under broiler until sugar is caramelized, about 5 seconds.) Serve immediately.

This warm, floral dessert combines the flavors and aromas of vanilla, sparkling wine, orange, honey, and roses—all things that remind me of the Spanish countryside.

serves 4

vanilla-soaked sponge cakes with rice sauce, cava gelée, orange-honey meringue, and rose air

* 1/2 cup rice sauce
* 4 vanilla-soaked sponge cakes
* 1/4 cup cava gelée
* 1/2 cup orange-honey meringue
* 1/4 cup rose air

*

rice sauce

Yields 1/2 cup

2 tablespoons bomba rice (see Sources and
    Substitutions)

1/2 cup water

2 tablespoons almonds, toasted

1/2 teaspoon unsalted butter

1 1/4 tablespoons granulated sugar

6 tablespoons whole milk

2 tablespoons heavy cream

• In a saucepan over medium heat, slowly
cook rice with water and almonds until
soft, 5 to 7 minutes. In a food processor,
combine rice mixture with remaining
ingredients. Puree until smooth and
creamy. Strain through a chinois, and cool.

*

vanilla-soaked sponge cakes

Yields 6 cakes

Unsalted butter, for pan

6 tablespoons all-purpose flour, plus flour
    for pan

1 large egg, separated

6 tablespoons granulated sugar

1/4 tablespoon baking powder

2 tablespoons whole milk

6 tablespoons vanilla simple syrup (see
    following recipe)

• Preheat oven to 325°F. Butter and flour 6
cups of a 12-cup muffin pan. Using an
electric mixer, whip egg white until frothy.
Slowly add sugar until a stiff meringue
forms. Whip in yolk.

• In a separate bowl, sift together flour
and baking powder. Add flour mixture and
milk in parts to egg mixture, whisking until
smooth.

• Evenly pour batter into 6 prepared
muffin cups. Bake until cakes have just
started to brown and feel slightly firm in
the center, about 20 minutes. When cakes
are cooled slightly, remove from pan and
cut out the center of each cake using an
apple corer. Holding each cake from the
bottom, invert in vanilla simple syrup and
soak the top half. Turn cakes upright.
Reserve 4 cakes. The other cakes can be
frozen in an airtight container for up to 2
weeks.

vanilla simple syrup

Yields 1 cup

1 cup granulated sugar

1 cup water

1 vanilla bean

• In a saucepan over high heat, boil sugar
and water for 2 minutes. Halve and scrape
out the seeds of the vanilla bean. Add
seeds and vanilla bean to syrup. Allow to sit
for at least 10 minutes. Remove vanilla
bean. Vanilla simple syrup can be
refrigerated for up to 1 month.

*

cava gelée

Yields 1/2 cup

1/2 sheet gelatin

6 3/4 tablespoons cava or other sparkling
wine

1 tablespoon granulated sugar

• In a bowl of ice water, bloom gelatin.
Squeeze out excess water. In a saucepan
over high heat, bring cava and sugar to a
boil. Add bloomed gelatin and stir until
dissolved. Chill until set, about 4 hours.
Gelée can be refrigerated for up to one
month.

*

orange-honey meringue

Yields 1 cup

1 large egg white

6 tablespoons granulated sugar

2 tablespoons clover honey

1/4 orange, zested

• Using an electric mixer, whip egg white
until soft peaks form. In a saucepan over
high heat, combine sugar and honey, and
boil until mixture reaches a temperature
of 238°F. Whisk hot syrup into whites; whip
until cool. Fold in orange zest. Meringue can
be stored in an airtight container in the
refrigerator for up to 4 days.

*

rose air

Yields about 1 cup

1 1/2 tablespoons grenadine

1 1/2 tablespoons rose water (see Sources
and Substitutions)

1/4 teaspoon rose syrup (see Sources and
Substitutions)

6 3/4 tablespoons water

3/4 tablespoon soy lecithin (see Sources
and Substitutions)

• In a bowl, mix together all ingredients
except lecithin. Add lecithin just before
using and buzz with a hand blender until a
stiff foam forms.

Putting it all together

• Spoon 2 tablespoons rice sauce on each
of 4 plates. Place a sponge cake in the
sauce and spoon 1 tablespoon cava gelée
into the center of each cake. Spoon 2
tablespoons orange-honey meringue on top
of each cake. Using a fork, pull the
meringue out in a ring from the center to
form a crown. Using a small brûlée torch,
lightly toast the meringue. (If you don't
have a blowtorch, preheat broiler. Place
meringue under broiler until toasted,
about 5 seconds.) Spoon 1 tablespoon rose
air into crown of each meringue. Serve
immediately.

Chocolate and bananas seem to be a universally popular dessert pairing. Here, I give the combination a Spanish twist with the addition of a fragrant saffron custard. Splinters of cocoa-almond brittle bring crunch to the soft, sweet caramelized bananas.

serves 4

caramel-rum bananas with flourless chocolate cake and saffron custard

* 1/4 cup saffron custard

* 4 servings chocolate cake

* 4 servings cocoa-almond brittle

* 12 pieces caramel-rum banana

* 1 cup caramel-rum sauce

  Pinch saffron, for garnish

*

saffron custard

Yields 1 1/4 cups

1/2 sheet gelatin

3/4 cup heavy cream

1/4 cup whole milk

1/4 cup granulated sugar

1/2 teaspoon saffron

1 large egg yolk

• In a bowl of ice water, bloom gelatin. Squeeze out excess water. In a saucepan over high heat, boil cream, milk, sugar, and saffron. In a separate bowl, whisk egg yolk. Whisk cream mixture into yolk to temper. Return mixture to saucepan over medium heat, and bring to 185°F, stirring constantly. Remove from heat and add bloomed gelatin. Stir until dissolved. Chill until set, about 3 hours. Custard can be stored in the refrigerator for up to 3 days.

*

chocolate cake

Yields 4 servings

2 3/4 tablespoons unsalted butter, plus butter for preparing pan

3 ounces semisweet chocolate

2 1/2 tablespoons water

2 tablespoons granulated sugar

1 large egg

• Preheat oven to 300°F. Prepare four 2-inch ring molds (at least 1 1/2 inches tall) by lining the bottom with aluminum foil to create pans. Make sure that the edges of foil reach almost to the top of the molds. Brush each with butter.

• In a double boiler, melt chocolate and butter, and whisk until smooth. In a saucepan over high heat, combine water and sugar, and boil 3 minutes to make simple syrup. Add syrup to melted chocolate. Whisk until smooth. Add egg and whisk until smooth.

• Pour 1/4 cup batter into each prepared pan. Place pans in a roasting pan and pour in enough hot water to come halfway up the side of the cake pans. Cover with aluminum foil and bake until cakes have just stopped moving in the center, 20 minutes. (Check cakes after 10 minutes and rotate in the oven.) Remove cake pans from water and refrigerate until completely set, about 1 hour. Remove cakes from pans and chill until ready to serve.

*

caramel-rum bananas and sauce

Yields 12 pieces and 1 1/4 cups sauce

1 cup granulated sugar

1/4 cup plus 1 tablespoon glucose syrup (see Sources and Substitutions)

1/2 cup water

1/4 cup dark rum

1 large banana

• In a saucepan over high heat, combine sugar, glucose syrup, and 1/4 cup water. Bring to a boil and continue cooking until sugar begins to caramelize. Remove from heat and add remaining 1/4 cup water and the rum. Be cautious, as caramel will spit when liquid is added. Return to heat and continue cooking until caramel reaches 219°F, about 10 minutes. Cool slightly.

• Prepare bananas about 30 minutes before serving. Peel banana and slice into 12 rounds; place in a sealable plastic bag. Add warm caramel to bananas and allow to sit for 15 to 20 minutes. Remove bananas and put remaining caramel in a saucepan. Reduce over high heat 3 to 4 minutes. Cool.

*

cocoa-almond brittle

Yields 4 servings

1/4 cup granulated sugar

1/4 cup water

1/2 cup sliced almonds

1/2 teaspoon extra-dark cocoa powder

• Preheat oven to 325°F. In a saucepan over high heat, cook sugar and water for 2 minutes to make simple syrup.

• In a bowl, combine almonds and cocoa powder. Add 2 tablespoons simple syrup. Stir until well coated. Spread almonds on a baking sheet lined with a nonstick, ovenproof sheet, such as a Silpat. Bake until sugar stops bubbling, 10 to 15 minutes. Brittle is done if it easily cracks apart when cooled. Cocoa-almond brittle can be stored in an airtight container at room temperature for up to 2 weeks.

putting it all together

• Smear a dollop of saffron custard on each of 4 chilled plates. Place one chocolate cake on each plate, and top with a piece of cocoa-almond brittle sticking out of the cake. Pile 3 bananas slices beside each cake, then drizzle bananas with 1/4 cup caramel-rum sauce. Garnish with crumbled cocoa-almond brittle and a few saffron threads.

Mato y miel—fresh goat's milk cheese from Catalonia and aromatic honey—is a classic Spanish dessert. This recipe borrows from that simple idea, molding the creamy cheese into a mousse and creating a sweet honey substitute out of oranges and olive oil.

serves 4

goat cheese mousse with orange-olive oil caramel, sweet potato chips, and orange blossom gelée

* 4 servings goat cheese mousse

* 1/4 cup orange-olive oil caramel

* 12 sweet potato chips

  12 orange segments

* 1/2 cup orange blossom gelée

*

orange–olive oil caramel

Yields 3/4 cup

1 cup orange juice

1/2 cup granulated sugar

2 1/2 tablespoons glucose syrup (see Sources and Substitutions)

1/4 cup water

2 tablespoons dark rum

2 tablespoons extra-virgin olive oil

• In a saucepan over high heat, reduce orange juice to 2 tablespoons. Set aside.

• In a saucepan over high heat, combine sugar, glucose syrup, and 2 tablespoons water. Bring to a boil and continue cooking until sugar begins to caramelize. Remove from heat and add remaining 2 tablespoons water and the rum. Be cautious, as caramel will spit when liquid is added. Return to heat and cook 5 minutes more. Cool slightly. Whisk orange juice reduction and olive oil into caramel. Cool completely.

*

goat cheese mousse

Yields 4 servings

2/3 sheet gelatin

1/4 cup granulated sugar

2 tablespoons whole milk

3 1/2 ounces fresh goat cheese

2 tablespoons crème fraîche

7 tablespoons heavy cream

• In a bowl of ice water, bloom gelatin. Squeeze out excess water. In a saucepan over high heat, cook sugar and milk until almost boiling. Add bloomed gelatin. Allow to cool but not set.

• In a food processor, puree goat cheese with crème fraîche. Pour milk mixture into goat cheese mixture and process until smooth. Pour into a bowl.

• In a separate bowl, whip cream to soft peaks using an electric mixer. Fold into goat cheese mixture.

• Pour into four 1/2-cup oval silicone molds and freeze, about 4 hours. Remove from molds and place on serving plates. Refrigerate until needed. Mousses need to sit in refrigerator for at least half an hour to defrost before serving.

✳

sweet potato chips

Yields about 20 chips

1/2 cup granulated sugar

1/2 cup water

1 small sweet potato

• Preheat oven to 300°F. In a saucepan over high heat, boil sugar and water for 2 minutes to make simple syrup. Cool slightly.

• Cut sweet potato into 1-inch-thick slices. Using a 2-inch round cutter cut out rounds. Using a mandoline slicer, slice very thin, almost transparent rounds of the sweet potato, to make at least 12 pieces.

• Place sweet potatoes in a microwave-proof bowl and pour syrup over potatoes. Cover with plastic and microwave 3 minutes. Lay sweet potato rounds on a nonstick ovenproof surface, such as a Silpat, and bake in the oven until chips have just started to darken, about 20 minutes. Cool and store in an airtight container.

✳

orange blossom gelée

Yields 1/2 cup

1 sheet gelatin

1/2 teaspoon orange-blossom water (see Sources and Substitutions)

1/2 cup plus 3 tablespoons water

1 orange, zested

1/2 sprig rosemary

• In a bowl of ice water, bloom gelatin. Squeeze out excess water.

• In a saucepan over high heat, heat orange-blossom water, water, and orange zest until almost boiling. Stir in bloomed gelatin. Strain out zest and then add rosemary. Allow to steep until cool but not set. Remove rosemary sprig and chill until set, about 2 hours.

putting it all together

• Place goat cheese mousse on each of 4 plates and drizzle with 1 tablespoon orange–olive oil caramel. Place 3 sweet potato chips into each goat cheese mousse. Fan 3 orange segments next to the mousse, and place dollops of the orange blossom gelée around the plate.

Cinnamony arroz con leche—or rice with milk—is probably the best-known Latin dessert. This is my modern take on the classic dish. Instead of the expected raisins, I've used currants. To brighten the sometimes-heavy dish, I've added lemon. And to enhance the cinnamon flavor, I've garnished the pudding with canela tuiles.

serves 4

arroz con leche with blackberry-currant compote, lemon confit, and canela tuiles

* 1/2 cup blackberry-currant compote
* 2 cups arroz con leche
* 1/4 cup lemon confit
* 8 canela tuiles

  4 mint leaves

*

arroz con leche

Yields 2 cups

1/3 cup bomba rice (see Sources and
   Substitutions)

3/4 cup water

3/4 cup whole milk

2 1/2 tablespoons granulated sugar

1 teaspoon ground canela (see Sources and
   Substitutions)

7 tablespoons condensed milk

1/4 cup dried black currants

• In a saucepan over high heat, combine rice
and water. Cover and heat until boiling.
Reduce heat to a simmer and cook,
covered, until water is completely
absorbed, 20 to 30 minutes. Pour milk,
sugar, and canela into pot. Stir
immediately. Add condensed milk and bring
to a boil. Using a rubber spatula, stir
constantly for 5 minutes making sure to
scrape the bottom of the pan. Remove
from heat and fold in currants. Pour into
an 8-inch metal pan and cover in plastic.
Chill until firm.

*

blackberry-currant compote

Yields 1/2 cup

1/4 cup dried black currants

2 tablespoons water

1 tablespoon granulated sugar

1/4 teaspoon lemon juice

1/2 cup blackberries

• In a bowl, combine currants and water.
Heat in a microwave until water is hot,
about 1 minute. Cover bowl and allow to
rest until currants have rehydrated, about
5 minutes. Discard water. In a food
processor, combine black currents and
remaining ingredients; puree until smooth.

*

canela tuiles

Yields 8 tuiles

1 cup granulated sugar

1 cup water

1 sheet phyllo dough

2 tablespoons ground canela (see Sources and Substitutions)

• Preheat oven to 325°F. In a saucepan over high heat, boil sugar and water 2 minutes to make simple syrup. Cool. Working quickly, generously brush phyllo dough with simple syrup. Sprinkle canela evenly over sheet. Cut into 8 equal pieces. Tightly wrap each piece of soaked phyllo dough around a skewer. Remove from skewer and place on a baking sheet lined with parchment. Bake until crisp, 15 to 20 minutes.

---

putting it all together

• Spoon 2 tablespoons blackberry compote into the bottom of four 1-cup glasses. Spoon 1/2 cup arroz con leche over compote. Spoon 1 tablespoon lemon confit over arroz con leche. Finish with 2 canela tuiles and a mint leaf.

*

lemon confit

Yields 1/2 cup

1/2 lemon

1/4 cup granulated sugar

1 teaspoon apple pectin (see Sources and Substitutions)

2 1/2 tablespoons lemon juice

• Fill a saucepan with water and bring to a boil. Remove peel from lemon and cut it into small dice. Using a strainer, place lemon peel in boiling water to blanch, 1 minute. Immediately remove from hot water and shock in an ice bath. Strain and reserve diced lemon peel.

• Combine sugar and apple pectin in a bowl. In a saucepan over high heat, bring lemon juice and diced lemon peel to a boil. Pour a small amount of boiling juice into bowl of sugar and pectin. Whisk until smooth and then add back to the pot. Stir until mixture begins to boil again and thickens. Cool.

This dessert crosses all borders. You'll find versions of this addictive "fried milk" in Spain and Mexico, as well as throughout South America and the Caribbean. I've added a sweet-and-sour edge to it with a thick butterscotch sauce and orange segments.

serves 6

leche frita
with butterscotch sauce
and oranges

4 cups vegetable oil, for frying

* 30 breaded leche frita cubes

* 6 tablespoons butterscotch sauce

12 orange segments

✳

leche frita cubes

Yields about 32 cubes

1 cup plus 2 1/2 tablespoons whole milk

1/2 cup plus 2 1/2 tablespoons granulated
  sugar

1 tablespoon unsalted butter

1 tablespoon plus 1/2 teaspoon ground
  canela (see Sources and Substitutions)

1/2 teaspoon ground star anise

1 3/4 tablespoons cornstarch

2 large egg yolks

2 cups all-purpose flour

4 large eggs, whisked

2 cups bread crumbs

• Line an 8-inch-by-4-inch loaf pan with
plastic wrap. In a saucepan over high heat,
combine 1 cup milk, sugar, butter, 1/2
teaspoon ground canela, and star anise.
Bring to a boil, then remove from heat.

• In a separate bowl, combine cornstarch,
remaining 2 1/2 tablespoons milk, and egg
yolks. Pour half of hot liquid into
cornstarch mixture. Whisk until smooth
then pour back into the pot. Whisk over
heat until boiling. When mixture has
thickened, pour into prepared cake pan
and cover with plastic. Refrigerate until
cool and firm, about 20 minutes. Remove
plastic, and invert leche frita onto a
cutting board. Cut into 1-inch cubes.

• When ready to serve, place 3 bowls in a
line. Place flour in first bowl, 4 whisked
eggs in second bowl, and bread crumbs
mixed with remaining 1 tablespoon ground
canela in third. Toss cubes in flour until
evenly coated. Toss floured cubes into eggs
and coat evenly. Shake off excess egg and
then toss cubes in bread crumbs. Place on
a tray. Breaded cubes can be frozen for
up to 3 weeks.

✳

butterscotch sauce

Yields 6 tablespoons

1/4 cup light brown sugar

1 1/4 tablespoons unsalted butter

1/4 cup heavy cream

1/2 teaspoon orange zest

1/4 teaspoon vanilla extract

1/4 tablespoon dark rum

• In a saucepan over high heat, heat all
ingredients, stirring until sugar and butter
are melted. Boil 2 to 3 minutes. Cool.

putting it all together

• Heat oil in a fryer or deep, heavy-
bottomed 4-quart pan to 350°F. Drop
breaded leche frita cubes 4 at a time into
oil and fry until golden brown, about 35
seconds. Scoop out onto paper towels.

• Spoon butterscotch sauce onto 6 plates.
Place 5 leche frita cubes in the sauce on
each plate. Top with orange segments.
Serve immediately.

basics

The first step in preparing any dish is having the right ingredients in your pantry. The recipes in this chapter are my kitchen staples. Though some of the oils, confits, pickles, and other recipes here can seem time-consuming, they're worth the effort. And many of them can be made in large amounts in advance and stored for later use. When storing these—or any other recipe in the book—vacuum sealing is the best option for preserving flavor, but a sealed plastic container is also a good choice.

oils

garlic oil (and roasted garlic)

Yields 2 cups oil and about 60 cloves

2 cups garlic cloves

2 cups grapeseed oil

• Preheat oven to 400°F. Place garlic and oil in a baking pan and cover tightly. Place pan in oven and cook until the garlic is golden brown, about 1 hour. Uncover and strain. Garlic oil can be refrigerated for up to 1 month. Roasted garlic can be refrigerated separately for up to 1 month.

lemon oil

Yields 4 cups

5 lemons, zested

4 cups grapeseed oil

1/4 cup turmeric

• Combine zest, oil, and turmeric in a saucepan and bring to a boil. Remove oil from heat and cool to room temperature. Strain through a chinois and chill. Lemon oil can be refrigerated for up to 2 weeks.

mustard oil

Yields 4 1/2 cups

4 cups grapeseed oil

3 tablespoons processed Dijon mustard

1/2 cup whole-grain Dijon mustard

1 tablespoon dried mustard

2 tablespoons turmeric

• In a saucepan, cook all ingredients over low heat for 30 minutes. Strain through a chinois and chill. Mustard oil can be refrigerated for up to 2 weeks.

oregano oil

Yields 2 cups

1/2 cup oregano leaves

2 cups grapeseed oil

1 1/2 cups flat-leaf parsley leaves

3 tablespoons chopped chives

1 cup baby spinach

• Roughly chop oregano and place in a saucepan with oil. Bring to a simmer; remove from heat and cool to room temperature. Combine all ingredients in a blender. Puree until smooth. Pass through a chinois, and chill in an ice bath. Whisk to chill oil quickly to preserve color. Oregano oil can be refrigerated for up to 2 weeks.

parsley oil

Yields 2 cups

2 1/4 cups flat-leaf parsley leaves

1/2 cup baby spinach

3 tablespoons chopped chives

2 cups grapeseed oil

• Heat oil to 275°F. In a blender, combine parsley, spinach, and chives, and slowly pour in oil while processing. Puree for 1 minute. Strain through a fine-mesh strainer. Chill in an ice bath to preserve color. Parsley oil can be refrigerated for up to 2 weeks.

red chile oil

Yields 2 cups

2 guajillo chiles, seeded (see Sources and Substitutions)

2 cups grapeseed oil

• In a saucepan, combine chiles and oil and cook over a low flame for 30 minutes. Add everything to a blender and puree smooth. Pass through a chinois. Red chile oil can be refrigerated for up to 3 months.

rosemary oil

Yields 1 1/2 cups

1 1/2 cups rosemary leaves

1 1/2 cups grapeseed oil

• In a saucepan, combine rosemary and oil and cook over a low flame for 30 minutes. Add everything to a blender and puree smooth. Pass through a chinois. Rosemary oil can be refrigerated for up to 3 months.

smoked paprika oil

Yields 2 cups

2 cups grapeseed oil

1/2 cup smoked sweet paprika (see Sources and Substitutions)

• In a saucepan, whisk together oil and paprika. Simmer over low heat for 30 minutes. Strain through a coffee filter and chill. Smoked paprika oil can be refrigerated for up to 1 month.

stocks

chicken stock

Yields about 16 cups

2 1/2 pounds chicken backs, cleaned of all fat and skin

4 cups chopped Spanish onion

1 leek, chopped

1 carrot, chopped

2 fresh bay leaves

9 sprigs thyme

5 cloves garlic

1 tablespoon black peppercorns

16 cups water

• Combine everything in a stockpot and cover with water. Bring to a boil; reduce to a simmer. Cook uncovered for 3 hours, skimming any foam that rises to the top. Strain out solids. Chicken stock can be refrigerated for up to 1 week or frozen for up to 3 months.

clam stock

Yields 16 cups

5 shallots, chopped

36 sprigs thyme

30 sprigs parsley

2 teaspoons red chile flakes

1/4 cup vegetable oil

4 cups white wine

10 Quahog chowder clams

16 cups water

• In a stockpot over low heat, sweat shallots, thyme, parsley, and chile flakes in vegetable oil until shallots are translucent. Add white wine and clams and bring to a boil. Add water and bring back to a boil.

Reduce to a simmer. Once the clams open, remove them and remove the meat from the shells. Chop the meat and store in the freezer for other uses, such as soup, chowder, or the littleneck clams with bomba rice dish in this book (see p. 177). Continue to cook the stock for an additional 20 minutes, uncovered; skim any foam that rises to the top. Strain out solids. Clam stock can be refrigerated for up to 1 week or frozen for up to 3 months.

clam velouté

Yields 2 1/2 cups

1/4 cup unsalted butter

1/4 cup all-purpose flour

2 cups clam stock (see previous recipe) or clam juice

• In a saucepan over medium heat, combine butter and flour, cooking until a blond color, about 4 minutes. Whisk in clam stock and simmer for 8 minutes. Clam velouté can be refrigerated for up to 1 day.

corn stock

Yields 4 cups

8 chopped corn cobs, kernels removed and reserved for other use

8 cups chopped Spanish onion

5 cloves garlic, chopped

8 cups water

• In a stockpot, combine all ingredients and bring to a boil. Reduce heat and simmer uncovered for 2 hours, skimming any foam that rises to the top. Strain through a chinois. Corn stock can be refrigerated for up to 1 week or frozen for up to 3 months.

shellfish stock

Yields 8 cups

1 1/2 pounds shellfish bodies (lobster, crab, or shrimp), gills removed

1/4 cup vegetable oil

4 cups chopped Spanish onion

1 stalk celery, chopped

1/2 bulb fennel, chopped

1 beefsteak tomato, chopped

1/2 cup tomato paste

12 cups water

• Preheat oven to 500°F. Place the shellfish bodies in a roasting pan and place in the oven. Cook shellfish bodies until bright red and fragrant, about 20 minutes.

• In a stockpot over a high flame, heat vegetable oil. Sauté onions, celery, and fennel until browned. Add tomatoes and cook for an additional 20 minutes, until fully cooked down. Add tomato paste and cook another 5 minutes. Add shellfish bodies and water. Over high heat, bring to a boil and then reduce to a light simmer. Cook uncovered for 1 1/2 hours, skimming any foam that rises to the top. Strain out solids and chill. Shellfish stock can be refrigerated for up to 1 week or frozen for up to 3 months.

veal stock

Yields 8 cups

5 pounds veal bones

1/2 cup tomato paste

7 1/2 cups chopped Spanish onions

3 carrots, chopped

2 1/2 gallons water

8 cups red wine

5 shallots, minced

• Preheat oven to 300°F. In a roasting pan, roast bones until dark brown. Remove bones from oven and rub with tomato paste. Return to oven and continue to roast until tomato paste is caramelized. Transfer bones to stockpot. Add onions and carrots to the roasting pan and roast until lightly caramelized. Transfer onions and carrots to a stockpot. Add water to the stockpot and bring to a boil. Reduce heat and simmer uncovered for 6 hours, skimming any foam or fat from the surface. Strain out solids. Return liquid to stockpot.

• In a stockpot over high heat, combine wine and shallots. Reduce mixture to a syrup. Add to veal stock.

• Bring stock to a boil and reduce to 8 cups. Stock can be refrigerated for up to 1 week or frozen for up to 2 months.

vegetable stock

Yields 4 cups

8 cups chopped Spanish onion

1 carrot, chopped

1 leek, chopped

3 cloves garlic

1/4 cup vegetable oil

1 bay leaf

1/2 bunch parsley

1 teaspoon white peppercorns

8 cups water

• In a stockpot over medium heat, sweat vegetables in vegetable oil until wilted. Add herbs, pepper, and water and bring to a boil. Reduce to a simmer and cook uncovered for 1 hour, skimming any foam that rises to the top. Strain out solids. Vegetable stock can be refrigerated for up to 1 week or frozen for up to 3 months.

white shrimp stock

Yields 4 cups

1 pound shrimp shells

4 cups chopped Spanish onion

2 stalks celery, chopped

1 carrot, chopped

1/2 bulb fennel, chopped

8 cups water

• Combine everything in a stockpot and bring to a boil over high heat. Reduce to a simmer and cook uncovered for 1 1/2 hours, skimming any foam that rises to the top. Strain out solids. White shrimp stock can be refrigerated for up to 1 week or frozen for up to 3 months.

vegetables

caramelized onions

Yield 1 cup

2 1/2 cups finely julienned Spanish onions
1/4 cup vegetable oil
2 tablespoons unsalted butter

• In a saucepan, combine all ingredients and cook over low heat for 3 hours, stirring often, until deep brown. Caramelized onions can be refrigerated for up to 2 weeks.

caramelized specialty onions

Pearl onions, red pearl onions, or cipollini onions can be used.

Yields 1 cup

1 tablespoon unsalted butter
1 cup onions, peeled
1 1/2 cups water
2 tablespoons granulated sugar

• In a sauté pan over a medium flame, heat butter. Add onions. Sauté until slightly browned. Add 1/2 cup water to deglaze pan. Add sugar and reduce water to almost dry. Repeat the deglazing two more times, adding 1/2 cup water each time, but no more sugar. Caramelized onions can be refrigerated for up to 2 weeks.

chile paste

Any type of chile can be used.

Yields 1 to 2 cups

8 cups vegetable oil, for frying
10 chiles
5 cloves roasted garlic

• In a fryer or deep heavy bottomed saucepan, heat vegetable oil to 350°F. Remove seeds and stems from chiles. Fry chiles for 5 seconds. Soak fried chiles in cold water 10 minutes. Remove chiles from water, reserving soaking liquid. Place in a blender with 1/2 cup soaking liquid and garlic. Puree until smooth. Chile paste can be refrigerated for up to 1 month.

confit artichokes

Yields 8 artichokes

5 cloves garlic
3 sprigs rosemary
6 sprigs thyme
8 artichokes, trimmed
2 tablespoons kosher salt
Vegetable oil, to cover

• Preheat oven to 300°F. Place all ingredients in a deep pan. Spread out garlic and herbs and make sure artichokes are completely submerged in oil. Cover tightly with aluminum foil and cook for 1 hour, until artichokes are tender. Place artichokes on a rack to drain, and cool at room temperature. When cool, clean artichokes by using a small spoon to scrape the choke from the center. Confit artichokes can be stored in oil for up to 6 months.

confit cherry tomatoes

Yields 2 cups

2 cups cherry tomatoes

4 cups extra-virgin olive oil

10 cloves garlic

4 sprigs rosemary

8 sprigs thyme

3 tablespoons kosher salt

• Preheat oven to 200°F. Cut a small X in the bottom of each tomato. Place all ingredients in a deep pan and cover tightly with aluminum foil. Cook for 1 hour, until tomatoes are tender and skin starts to pull away. Peel the skins back halfway but do not pull them off. Confit cherry tomatoes can be refrigerated in oil for up to 6 months.

confit potatoes

Yukon Gold potatoes or purple Peruvian potatoes can be used.

Yields 12 slices

4 potatoes, peeled

5 cloves garlic

6 sprigs rosemary

10 sprigs thyme

4 cups extra-virgin olive oil

3 tablespoons kosher salt

• Preheat oven to 300°F. Using a 1-inch ring cutter, cut a cylinder from each potato, and slice cylinders into 1/4-inch-thick coins. In a cast-iron pan, combine all ingredients. Cover tightly and bake until tender, about 1 hour. Strain oil if using immediately, and discard garlic and herbs. Arrange potatoes in a single layer to cool. Confit potatoes can be refrigerated in its oil for up to 1 month.

garlic chips

Yields 1 cup

15 cloves garlic

1/2 cup coconut milk

2 cups vegetable oil

Kosher salt, to taste

• Cut off the bottom of each clove of garlic. On a mandolin very thinly slice garlic, and add slices to coconut milk. Marinate garlic for 1 hour. Drain through a mesh strainer. (Do not wash garlic.)

• In a sauté pan, add oil and gently heat to about 275°F. (Drop a piece of the garlic into the oil to check for the right temperature. Oil should just slightly start to bubble.) Turn heat to low and add garlic, stirring. Keep stirring so garlic cooks evenly. When garlic begins to color, remove with a slotted spoon to paper towels to drain. Garlic will continue to color as it dries and crisps. Season with salt. Garlic chips can be stored at room temperature in an airtight container, with a paper towel to absorb moisture, for up to 3 weeks.

onion confit

Spanish onions or red onions can be used.

Yields 5 cups

3 onions, peeled

8 cups extra-virgin olive oil

2 sprigs rosemary

2 sprigs thyme

• In a saucepan, combine onions, oil, and herbs. Over medium-low heat, cook the onions until extremely tender, about 10 hours. Chill. Remove herbs. In a food processor, puree until smooth. Onion confit can be refrigerated for up to 1 month.

pickled jalapeño chile rings

Yields 2 cups chile rings

10 jalapeño chiles, sliced into very thin rings

2 shallots, sliced thin

4 bay leaves

1/2 cup dried oregano

1/2 cup dried thyme

1/4 cup black peppercorns

1 cup kosher salt

1 cup granulated sugar

4 cups white vinegar

4 cups water

• Combine all ingredients. Allow to pickle in the refrigerator for at least 24 hours. Pickled jalapeños can be refrigerated in a plastic container for up to 1 month.

roasted corn

Yields 1 cup

1 cup corn kernels

1 tablespoon vegetable oil

• In a sauté pan over high heat, sauté corn kernels in vegetable oil until lightly browned. Roasted corn can be refrigerated for up to 1 week.

roasted garlic

See Garlic Oil recipe, p. 267.

roasted mushrooms

Any type and quantity of mushroom can be used.

Mushrooms

Extra-virgin olive oil, to coat

Kosher salt, to taste

Black pepper, to taste

• Preheat oven to 350°F. Toss mushrooms in olive oil to lightly coat. Season with salt and pepper. Roast for 6 minutes. Mushrooms can be refrigerated for up to 1 week.

roasted peppers and chiles

Any type and quantity of bell pepper or fresh chile can be used.

Bell peppers or chiles

Vegetable oil, to coat

• Preheat oven to 500°F. Remove stems and seeds and toss peppers or chiles in vegetable oil to lightly coat. Roast until skin is slightly blackened and blistered. Remove from oven, place in a container, and cover tightly for 5 to 10 minutes. Remove from the container and peel off skins. Roasted peppers and chiles can be refrigerated for up to 2 weeks.

roasted plum tomatoes

Any quantity of plum tomato can be used.

Plum tomatoes

Vegetable oil, to coat

Kosher salt, to taste

Black pepper, to taste

• Preheat an oven to 375°F. Cut tomatoes into quarters and toss with vegetable oil to lightly coat. Season with salt and pepper. Roast for 30 minutes. Roasted tomatoes can be refrigerated for up to 2 weeks.

sauces, creams, and marinades

adobo marinade

Yields 1 1/2 cups

2 cloves garlic

1/4 cup lard

5 teaspoons thyme leaves

2 1/2 tablespoons oregano leaves

1 clove

2 allspice berries

1/2 stick canela (see Sources and Substitutions)

1 teaspoon black peppercorns

1 tablespoon guajillo chile paste (see Basics, p. 272)

1 tablespoon pasilla chile paste (see Basics, p. 272)

1/2 cup apple cider vinegar

1/2 cup water

Kosher salt, to taste

Black pepper, to taste

• In a saucepan, sauté garlic in lard until browned, being very careful not to burn the garlic. Add thyme, oregano, clove, allspice, canela, peppercorns, and guajillo and pasilla chile pastes to saucepan. Toast 5 minutes. Add vinegar and water. Bring liquid to a boil over high heat then reduce to a simmer. Reduce by 1/4. In a blender, puree mixture until smooth. Season to taste with salt and pepper. Adobo marinade can be refrigerated for up to 2 weeks.

béchamel

Yields 2 cups

1/4 cup plus 1 tablespoon unsalted butter

1/4 cup plus 1 tablespoon all-purpose flour

1 1/2 cups whole milk

Kosher salt, to taste

• In a saucepan, melt butter over low heat. With a rubber spatula, stir in flour. Continue to cook over low heat for 2 minutes, stirring several times. Stir in half the milk, cooking over low heat until mixture thickens, about 5 minutes. Stir in remaining milk. Continue to cook over low heat stirring regularly until smooth. Season with salt. Béchamel can be refrigerated for up to 1 week.

crema mexicana

Yields 1 cup

1 cup crème fraîche

2 limes, juiced

1 teaspoon kosher salt

2 tablespoons heavy cream

• In a bowl, combine crème fraîche and lime juice. Add salt and cream and stir until thoroughly mixed. Crema Mexicana can be refrigerated for up to 1 week.

sauce basquaise

Yields 4 cups

4 cups chopped Spanish onion

3 cloves garlic, crushed

1 tablespoon vegetable oil

1 red bell pepper, chopped

1 green bell pepper, chopped

1/2 tablespoon espelette powder (see Sources and Substitutions)

2 1/2 tablespoons choricero chile paste (see Basics, p. 272)

4 sprigs thyme, tied together

4 plum tomatoes, chopped

2 teaspoons kosher salt

• In a saucepan over medium heat, sauté onions and garlic in vegetable oil until onions are tender. Add peppers and continue to sauté until peppers are tender. Add espelette powder, choricero paste, and thyme. Cook 5 more minutes. Add tomatoes and cook over medium heat for 1 hour, stirring frequently. Remove thyme and puree mixture with a hand blender until smooth. Season with salt, and place into refrigerator to cool. Sauce Basquaise can be refrigerated for up to 1 week.

standard aïoli

Yields 1 cup

3 egg yolks

1 clove garlic, zested

1/4 lemon, juiced

2/3 cup vegetable oil

Kosher salt, to taste

• Combine egg yolks, garlic, and lemon juice in a food processor and puree smooth. While processing, slowly add oil to emulsify. Season with salt. Aïoli can be refrigerated for up to 1 week.

standard ceviche marinade

Yields 1 1/3 cups

2 jalapeño chiles, brunoised

1/4 cup extra-virgin olive oil

2 tablespoons finely chopped cilantro

8 limes, juiced

• Combine all ingredients. Use immediately.

standard romesco sauce

Yields 2 cups

1/2 cup almonds

1 cup roasted plum tomatoes (see Basics, p. 273)

1 cup roasted red bell peppers (see Basics, p. 273)

2 cloves roasted garlic (see Basics, p. 267)

2 teaspoons honey

2 tablespoons sherry vinegar

1/4 teaspoon red pepper flakes

1/2 cup extra-virgin olive oil

Kosher salt, to taste

• Preheat oven to 375°F. Arrange almonds on a sheet tray and bake until light golden brown. In a food processor, combine tomatoes, bell peppers, garlic, honey, vinegar, and red pepper flakes. Puree until smooth. Add toasted almonds and process. While processing, slowly add olive oil. The sauce should be slightly chunky. Season with salt.

seafood, poultry, and meats

confit duck legs

Yields 6 duck legs

6 sticks canela (see Sources and
Substitutions)

2 tablespoons star anise

1 tablespoon cloves

4 cups kosher salt

1 navel orange, sliced

6 duck legs

3 pounds duck fat

• In a bowl, combine spices, salt, and orange slices. Trim duck legs of excess fat. In a pan, spread half of spice mixture. Lay duck legs in one layer on top and cover with remaining spice mixture. Be sure to completely cover duck legs. Wrap tightly and refrigerate overnight.

• Preheat oven to 200°F. Remove duck legs from spice mixture and gently wash legs, removing any salt or spices that may have stuck to them, to stop the curing process. Place duck legs in a deep pan and cover with duck fat. Cover tightly with aluminum foil. Cook until the bones fall out of the meat, about 8 hours. Refrigerate to cool. Confit duck legs can be refrigerated in duck fat for up to 1 year.

dried serrano ham

Yields 3 pieces

3 ounces serrano ham

• Preheat oven to 200°F. Cut ham into three 2-inch cubes. Place ham on a baking sheet and cook for 8 hours. Ham can be refrigerated for up to 1 month.

foie gras torchon

Yields 1/2 pound torchon

3/4 pound foie gras lobe

4 cups whole milk

2 tablespoons brandy

1 tablespoon sea salt

1/2 tablespoon black pepper

2 1/2 pounds clarified butter

• In a bowl, soak foie gras in milk for 2 hours at room temperature. Remove foie gras from milk and pat dry. Discard milk. Devein foie gras, starting in the middle of the lobe. Try to keep the lobe in one piece. Clean foie gras of all blemishes. Sprinkle with brandy, salt, and pepper. Roll foie gras in a 2-foot-by-1-foot piece of cheesecloth until foie gras is a long cylinder about 2 inches in diameter. Twist cheesecloth ends and tie tightly. (Some foie gras should squeeze out.) Hang in refrigerator overnight.

• In a deep baking pan, heat clarified butter to 180°F. Add foie gras in cheesecloth and poach for 10 minutes. Remove foie gras and reshape as needed. Hang in refrigerator overnight. Foie gras torchon can be stored in cheesecloth, hanging in refrigerator, for up to 3 weeks.

poached lobster

or poached spot prawns

Yields 2 poached lobsters (1/2 pound meat) or 12 spot prawns

1/2 cup pickling spice

2 lemons, quartered

5 cloves garlic, chopped

16 cups water

1/2 cup kosher salt

2 lobsters (1 to 1 1/4 pounds each) or 12 spot prawns

• In a sauté pan over medium heat, toast pickling spice, 1 to 2 minutes. In a stockpot, bring all ingredients except lobster or prawns to a boil over high heat.

• If using lobster, break off the claws and tail sections of lobster. Run a small skewer through the tail between the meat and the shell along the bottom of the tail to keep tail straight. Drop claws and tail pieces into the stock and turn off the heat. Remove the tails after 4 minutes and the claws after 8 minutes. Shock in ice water. Crack the claws and remove the meat. Poached lobster meat can be refrigerated for up to 2 days.

• If using prawns, peel and devein prawns. Drop prawns into stock and turn off heat. Remove prawns after 2 minutes. Shock in ice water. Poached prawns can be refrigerated for up to 2 days.

serrano ham chips

Yields 3 to 4 ounces

2 ounces serrano ham, thinly sliced

• Preheat oven to 250°F. On a nonstick ovenproof surface, such as a Silpat, arrange ham slices in a single layer and place on a sheet tray. Cover with another Silpat. Cook for 20 minutes, until ham is almost but not completely dried. Uncover and cool. (Chips will harden as they cool.) Ham chips can be stored in an airtight container for up to 4 days.

serrano ham fat

Yields 1/2 cup

1/4 pound serrano ham trimmings

1/2 cup grapeseed oil

• Preheat oven to 250°F. In a deep baking pan, combine trimmings and oil. Cover tightly with aluminum foil and cook for 2 hours. Strain oil, discarding trimmings. Serrano ham fat can be refrigerated for up to 2 weeks.

miscellaneous

preserved lemons

Yields 40 slices

1 cup kosher salt

1 tablespoon saffron

4 cups vegetable oil

5 sprigs thyme

5 lemons, sliced into 1/4-inch rings

• In a saucepan over medium heat, combine salt, saffron, oil, and thyme. Pour mixture over lemons, and set aside to cool. Preserved lemons can be refrigerated up to 1 month.

simple syrup

Use for granulated sugar or invert sugar.

Yields 1 cup

1 cup water

1 cup sugar

• In a saucepan, combine water and sugar and stir until sugar is dissolved. Place saucepan over low heat and cook until the liquid becomes clear. Simple syrup can be refrigerated for up to 1 month.

sous vide

The sous-vide cooking method is excellent for preserving flavors, aromas, and nutrients. Additionally, because of the combination of heat and pressure, varied textures can be produced—meats can be made tender; eggs, custard like; and vegetables, surprisingly dense. In sous-vide cooking, foods are typically packaged inside airtight or vacuum-sealed plastic bags and cooked in a water bath at a constant low temperature (below boiling) for a longer period of time than used in most cooking methods.

A few important guidelines: To ensure food safety, cook foods immediately after packaging. Use a circulator to maintain a constant temperature, which is also essential for food safety. If using a water bath, keep a thermometer submerged to monitor temperature.

Time, temperature, and pressure variations will have different effects on different foods. For more information, consult *Sous-Vide Cuisine* by Joan Roca and Salvador Brugues (Montagud Editores, 2005).

tortillas and mini tostadas

Yields about 20 (4-inch) tortillas or about 80 mini tostadas

1 cup plus 3 tablespoons water

1 pound masa harina

2 tablespoons vegetable oil, plus more for frying

2 teaspoons red chile flakes

2 tablespoons kosher salt

• Mix water, masa harina, 2 tablespoons vegetable oil, chile flakes, and salt together in a bowl until a dough forms. Roll dough into 2-tablespoon balls and press into rounds in a tortilla press lined with plastic wrap.

• For tortillas: Heat 1 tablespoon vegetable oil in a cast-iron pan over medium heat. Add a dough round and cook until lightly browned. Flip and brown the other side. Continue with remaining dough, adding 1 tablespoon oil with each dough round. Use immediately.

• For tostadas: In a fryer or deep, heavy-bottomed 4-quart pan, heat 4 cups vegetable oil to 350°F. Cut dough rounds into little triangles and fry until crisp, about 1 minute. Drain. Use immediately.

sources

& substitutions

The recipes in this cookbook span the globe, from the Basque region of Spain to the coast of Peru to Buenos Aires, Argentina. But thanks to the Internet, even the most regional ingredients are available around the world. Check your local sources first. You'll be surprised at how well-stocked supermarkets and health food stores are today. The most difficult-to-find items will be the Spanish meats and Spanish and Mexican cheeses that are not yet imported in mass quantities. For those products I turn to La Española Meats (laespanolameats.com), Artisanal Premium Cheese (artisanalcheese.com), and Forever Cheese (forevercheese.com). I've listed my other favorite sources below. Sometimes an ingredient is essential to a dish—squid ink for your squid ink sauce, for instance—but in other cases, I've listed substitutes that are almost as good. If you find squid ink but no chipirones for that classic Basque dish, calamari is a delicious stand-in.

acacia honey

• what it is: A clear, delicate honey with vanilla and floral aromas and a liquid, even runny, texture
• where to find it: L'Epicerie (lepicerie.com)
• what to use instead: Any raw honey

achiote

• what it is: A brick-red paste originally from the Yucatán with a mild flavor; made from the seeds of the annatto tree and other spices
• where to find it: Local Latin groceries

agave nectar

• what it is: A Mexican product made from the juice of the agave plant; sweeter and thinner than most honeys
• where to find it: Local health food or organic food stores
• what to use instead: Any type of common honey

ají amarillo chiles

• what they are: Fruity, pungent yellow-orange chiles, common in Peru
• where to find them: Local latin groceries
• what to use instead: Anaheim chiles, which are similar in flavor but lack the vibrant color

almond flour

• what it is: Ground blanched almonds
• where to find it: Local health food or organic food stores
• what to use instead: Make your own flour, processing blanched almonds in a food processor in small batches until ground

amarena fabbri cherries

• what they are: Small, deep red, slightly sour Italian cherries packaged in a sugar syrup
• where to find them: Di Bruno Bros (dibruno.com)

ancho chiles

• what they are: Slightly sweet, deep red chiles; a dried version of the poblano chile
• where to find them: Local Latin groceries
• what to use instead: Other mild dried chiles, like guajillo and pasilla

apple pectin

• what it is: A pale powder derived from apples; used to thicken jams, jellies, and preserves
• where to find it: Local health food or organic food stores

arbequina olive oil

• what it is: Sweet, fruity, creamy oil pressed from the small, greenish brown arbequina olive, native to Spain
• where to find it: Despaña Brand Foods (despanabrandfoods.com), La Tienda (tienda.com), or Olé Olé (oleolefoods.com)
what to use instead: Any high-quality extra-virgin olive oil

avocado leaves

• what they are: The slightly anise-scented leaves of the avocado plant
• where to find them: Local Latin groceries

bacalao

• what it is: Dried salted cod that must be soaked in water before use; common in Spanish cooking
• where to find it: Despaña Brand Foods (despanabrandfoods.com) or La Tienda (tienda.com)

banana leaves

• what they are: The fibrous leaves of the banana tree; used for wrapping food but not typically eaten
• where to find them: In the frozen section of local Latin groceries

black truffle oil

• what it is: Oil infused with the aroma of black truffles
• where to find it: L'Epicerie (lepicerie.com)

black truffle peels

• what they are: The exterior of hard shell black truffles; used for flavoring
• where to find them: L'Epicerie (lepicerie.com)
• what to use instead: Black trumpet mushrooms

black truffles

• what they are: Pungent, earthy black fungi that grow at the roots of certain trees; highly prized in French and Italian cooking
• where to find them: Di Bruno Bros (dibruno.com)

black trumpet mushrooms

• what they are: Trumpet-shaped mushrooms from the chanterelle family, with a smoky aroma and buttery texture; available both fresh and dried
• where to find them: R. L. Irwin Mushroom Company (610-444-3800)

blue foot mushrooms

• what they are: Violet-tinged mushrooms with a strong flavor
• where to find them: R. L. Irwin Mushroom Company (610-444-3800)

bomba rice

• what it is: A short-grain rice grown in Spain's Calasparra region, capable of absorbing large amounts of liquid while maintaining its shape; often used in paella
• where to find it: Despaña Brand Foods (despanabrandfoods.com), La Tienda (tienda.com), or Olé Olé (oleolefoods.com)
• what to use instead: Italian-grown arborio rice

cachucha chiles

• what they are: Mild, sweet Cuban chiles similar in shape to habaneros, but without the heat
• where to find them: Local Latin groceries

canela

• what it is: Mexican cinnamon, with a sweeter taste and softer texture than the cinnamon commonly available in the United States
• where to find it: Local Latin groceries
• what to use instead: Common cinnamon

chile de arbol powder

• what it is: A tannic powder with lots of heat made from the popular Mexican red chile de arbol
• where to find it: Local Latin groceries

chipirones

• what they are: Baby squid; used in Spanish cooking
• where to find them: Local Asian markets
• what to use instead: Calamari

citric acid

• what it is: A granular powdered form of the acid that naturally occurs in citrus fruits; used as a preservative and to prevent discoloration
• where to find it: Local health food or organic food stores

culantro leaves

• what they are: A green herb used throughout Latin American and Asia; different in appearance but similar in pungent aroma to cilantro
• where to find them: Local Latin groceries or Asian markets
• what to use instead: Cilantro

dried lavender

• what it is: Dried flowers with a pronounced floral aroma; used to flavor sweet and savory dishes
• where to find it: Le Sanctuaire (le-sanctuaire.com)
• what to use instead: A vanilla bean

epazote

• what it is: A leafy green found in many Mexican dishes, with a strong licorice flavor
• where to find it: Local Latin groceries

espelette powder

• what it is: A powder made from the Basque region's espelette chile, with an intense, complex, spicy flavor
• where to find it: L'Epicerie (lepicerie.com)
• what to use instead: Ground cayenne pepper

fideo pasta

• what it is: A thin noodle found in Spanish and Mexican cooking; can be short or long in length.
• where to find it: Despaña Brand Foods (despanabrandfoods.com), La Tienda (tienda.com), or Olé Olé (oleolefoods.com)
• what to use instead: Dried angel-hair pasta (broken into pieces if substituting for short fideo)

foie gras mousse

• what it is: A cooked foie gras dish made with heavy cream
• where to find it: D'Artagnan (dartagnan.com)

glucose syrup

• what it is: A liquid sweetener similar to corn syrup but with a thicker consistency
• where to find it: Le Sanctuaire (le-sanctuaire.com)
• what to use instead: Corn syrup

guajillo chiles

• what they are: A rich, smoky, dried red chile common in Mexican cooking
• where to find them: Local Latin groceries,
• what to use instead: Other mild dried chiles, such as pasilla

guindilla chiles

• what they are: Long, dried red chiles popular in Spanish tapas, with a medium-hot flavor
• where to find them: Despaña Brand Foods (despanabrandfoods.com), La Tienda (tienda.com), or Olé Olé (oleolefoods.com)
• what to use instead: Other dried chiles, such as milder Mexican guajillo and pasilla chiles

guindilla chiles, pickled

• what they are: A pickled version of the dried Spanish chile
• where to find them: Despaña Brand Foods (despanabrandfoods.com) or La Tienda (tienda.com)
• what to use instead: Italian pepperoncini chiles

huacatay

• what it is: An herb known as Peruvian black mint, with a strong fragrance; available fresh and as a paste
• where to find it: Latin Merchant (latinmerchant.com)

huitlacoche

• what it is: A corn fungus with a mushroomy, earthy flavor; used in Mexican recipes
• where to find it: Local Latin groceries or Latin Merchant (latinmerchant.com)

ibarra chocolate

• what it is: A brand of Mexican dark chocolate flavored with cinnamon and sugar; often sold in thick disks
• where to find it: Local Latin groceries
• what to use instead: Any dark, almost bitter, chocolate

instant arepas flour

• what it is: A corn flour popular throughout Latin America
• where to find it: Local Latin groceries

invert sugar

• what it is: A product that is less sweet than granulated sugar; used to adjust texture
• where to find it: L'Epicerie (lepicerie.com)
• what to use instead: Granulated sugar

juniper berries

• what they are: A spice harvested from coniferous trees, with a fresh, piney flavor; a principle ingredient in gin
• where to find them: Le Sanctuaire (le-sanctuaire.com)

kobe tenderloin

• what it is: A high-quality, well-marbled beef from the Japanese Wagyu cow
• where to find it: Snake River Farms (snakeriverfarms.com)
• what to use instead: Prime American beef tenderloin

masa harina

• what it is: Dried corn flour; a staple in Mexican cooking, used in items like tortillas
• where to find it: Local Latin groceries

mexican oregano

• what it is: An aromatic, slightly bitter dried herb similar in flavor to common oregano
• where to find it: Local Latin groceries
• what to use instead: Common dried oregano

mojama

• what it is: Spanish salt-cured tuna loin
• where to find it: Despaña Brand Foods
(despanabrandfoods.com) or Olé Olé
(oleolefoods.com)

mulatto chiles

• what they are: An almost-black dried chile
with a mild, earthy flavor; popular in
Mexican recipes
• where to find them: Local Latin groceries
• what to use instead: Other mild dried
chiles like guajillo and pasilla

orange blossom water

• what it is: A floral liquid distilled from
orange blossoms; common in North African
cooking
• where to find it: Local Middle Eastern
groceries

palm oil

• what it is: A red cooking oil derived from
the fruit of the palm tree; popular in
African cooking
• where to find it: Local Asian or African
markets
• what to use instead: Vegetable oil, though
it lacks the vibrant color

pasilla chiles

• what they are: A long, black dried version
of the chilaca chile with a mild, earthy
flavor; common in Mexican mole
preparations
• where to find them: Local Latin groceries
• what to use instead: Other mild dried
chiles, like guajillo

pedro ximénez vinegar

• what it is: A sweet-sour sherry vinegar
aged in wood
• where to find it: Despaña Brand Foods
(despanabrandfoods.com), La Tienda
(tienda.com)
• what to use instead: Any high-quality
aged sherry vinegar

pepitas

• what they are: Pumpkin seeds; ground to
thicken Mexican sauces like pipián
• where to find them: Health food or
organic food stores

pink curing salt

• what it is: A salt-based mixture used in
the curing of sausages
• where to find it: Le Sanctuaire (le-
sanctuaire.com)

piquillo chiles

• what they are: Small Spanish chiles with a
spicy-sweet flavor
• where to find them: Despaña Brand Foods
(despanabrandfoods.com), La Tienda
(tienda.com), or Olé Olé (oleolefoods.com)

popcorn shoots

• what they are: Tender, vibrantly yellow
micro-greens with a sweet corn flavor and
a tangy aftertaste; produced from
popcorn seeds
where to find them: Blue Moon Acres
(bluemoonacres.net)

powdered agar

• what it is: A flavorless substance derived from seaweed that gels more firmly and at a higher temperature than gelatin
• where to find it: Local health food or organic food stores or Le Sanctuaire (lesanctuaire.com)

rose syrup

• what it is: A rose-infused sugar syrup; used in desserts and cocktails
• where to find it: Local Middle Eastern groceries

rose water

• what it is: Water distilled with roses; used in desserts and cocktails, especially in Asian and Middle Eastern cuisines
• where to find it: Local Middle Eastern groceries

royal trumpet mushrooms

• what they are: A versatile mushroom with delicate flavor and a tender cap and stem
• where to find them: R. L. Irwin Mushroom Company (610-444-3800)

smoked paprika

• what it is: Ground smoke-dried Spanish chiles labeled dulce, agridulce, or picante (indicating levels of heat and bitterness).
• where to find it: Despaña Brand Foods (despanabrandfoods.com), La Tienda (tienda.com), or Olé Olé (oleolefoods.com)
• what to use instead: Common paprika

soy lecithin

• what it is: A substance derived from soybean oil that acts as an emulsifier
• where to find it: Health food or organic food stores

squid ink

• what it is: A black liquid from the ink sacks of squid, popular in the Basque region; used to add a salty flavor and deep black color to sauces and rice
• where to find it: Despaña Brand Foods (despanabrandfoods.com) or La Tienda (tienda.com)

ventresca tuna

• what it is: The buttery belly of the tuna, sold canned, packed in olive oil
• where to find it: Despaña Brand Foods (despanabrandfoods.com), La Tienda (tienda.com), or Olé Olé (oleolefoods.com)
• what to use instead: High-quality canned tuna

xanthan gum

• what it is: A food additive produced through the fermentation of glucose or sucrose; used to add viscosity to a substance
• where to find it: Health food or organic food stores

yucca flour

• what it is: A flour made from yucca, a starchy vegetable, also known as manioc and cassava; common throughout Latin America
• where to find it: Latin Merchant (latinmerchant.com)

index